WHY ARE WE STILL DOING THAT?

Why Are We Still Doing That?

Positive Alternatives to Problematic Teaching Practices

Pérsida Himmele and William Himmele

Alexandria, Virginia USA

1703 N. Beauregard St. • Alexandria, VA 22311-1714 USA
Phone: 800-933-2723 or 703-578-9600 • Fax: 703-575-5400
Website: www.ascd.org • Email: member@ascd.org
Author guidelines: www.ascd.org/write

Ranjit Sidhu, *CEO & Executive Director;* Penny Reinart, *Chief Impact Officer;* Genny Ostertag, *Senior Director, Acquisitions and Editing;* Julie Houtz, *Director, Book Editing;* Katie Martin, *Editor;* Thomas Lytle, *Creative Director;* Donald Ely, *Art Director;* Keith Demmons, *Senior Production Designer;* Kelly Marshall, *Production Manager;* Christopher Logan, *Senior Production Specialist;* Shajuan Martin, *E-Publishing Specialist*

PAPERBACK ISBN: 978-1-4166-3051-7   ASCD product #122010
PDF E-BOOK ISBN: 978-1-4166-3052-4; see Books in Print for other formats.
Quantity discounts are available: email programteam@ascd.org or call 800-933-2723, ext. 5773, or 703-575-5773. For desk copies, go to www.ascd.org/deskcopy.

ASCD Member Book No. FY22-1 (September 2021 PSI+). ASCD Member Books mail to Premium (P), Select (S), and Institutional Plus (I+) members on this schedule: Jan, PSI+; Feb, P; Apr, PSI+; May, P; Jul, PSI+; Aug, P; Sep, PSI+; Nov, PSI+; Dec, P. For current details on membership, see www.ascd.org/membership.

Library of Congress Cataloging-in-Publication Data
Names: Himmele, Pérsida, author. | Himmele, William, author.
Title: Why are we still doing that? : positive alternatives to problematic teaching practices / Pérsida Himmele, William Himmele.
Description: Alexandria, VA : ASCD, [2021] | Includes bibliographical references and index.
Identifiers: LCCN 2021022035 (print) | LCCN 2021022036 (ebook) | ISBN 9781416630517 (paperback) | ISBN 9781416630524 (pdf)
Subjects: LCSH: Effective teaching. | School improvement programs.
Classification: LCC LB1025.3 .H545 2021 (print) | LCC LB1025.3 (ebook) | DDC 371.102--dc23
LC record available at https://lccn.loc.gov/2021022035
LC ebook record available at https://lccn.loc.gov/2021022036

30 29 28 27 26 25 24 23 22 21   1 2 3 4 5 6 7 8 9 10 11 12

To the educators who served during the COVID-19 pandemic—the ones who stayed, the ones who left, and the ones we lost.

WHY ARE WE STILL DOING THAT?

Introduction

"Houston, we have a problem."
Apollo 13, 1995

We, Pérsida and Bill, have been in the field of education for 30 years. How long is 30 years? It's long enough to have watched school boards sheepishly back away from mandates requiring female teachers to wear pantyhose with their dresses and skirts. It's long enough to remember walking out of the teachers' lounge smelling like a pack of Marlboros. Thirty years is long enough to have seen educational trends come, go, and then come back around again. And it's long enough to have gained sufficient perspective to say that some things in education haven't changed a bit.

We've also been married for 30 years, and we work in the same university, in the same department, and in offices two doors down from each other. On our ride home in the evening, we'll talk about our day. Often, we talk about the amazing teachers with whom we work. And some days, after spending the morning pointing out the problems with ineffective or inadvertently damaging educational practices and the afternoon visiting schools where those very same practices are still alive and well, we'll say to each other, *"Why are we still doing that?"* In other words, why do instructional, assessment, and classroom management practices that we know to be counterproductive nevertheless stay in place year after year?

The answer we gravitate to is a simple one: old habits die hard, particularly when they are part of what Dylan Wiliam (2007) calls the unexamined "scripts" of schooling. Most teachers spend about 13,000 hours in the classroom as students before they graduate high school. That's a lot of hours soaking up habits that they will later consciously or unconsciously perpetuate, even after learning about best practices in college or university. "Teachers learn most of what they know about teaching before they are 18 years old," writes Wiliam. He continues:

> In the same way that most of us learn what we know about parenting through being parented, teachers have internalized the "scripts" of school from when they themselves were students. Even the best 4-year teacher-education programs will find it hard to overcome the models of practice their future teachers learned in the 13 or 14 years they spend in school as students. (p. 196)

This book is about looking closely at those old scripts, seeing how they really play out today, and recommending many for retirement. We delve into familiar habits across the range of education practice (instruction, assessment, lesson design, and classroom management) that the research identifies as problematic and suggest positive alternatives that better support student growth.

A Critical Clarification

Pérsida used to be a telemarketer. Every Sunday night for more than a year, she'd find her stomach tied in knots at the prospect of another grueling workweek spent cold-calling unfriendly strangers. Even getting somewhat good at it didn't alleviate the worry; as anyone who's done it can attest, telemarketing is brutal work. But teaching is arguably harder—in a keep-you-up-at-night, never-forget-your-worst-mistakes kind of way. It's the type of work that can mess with your head. When Pérsida had a bad day as a telemarketer, she felt like a bad telemarketer; when she had a bad day as a teacher, she felt like a bad *person*. You can have 179 good days in a school year, but it's that one bad day that you'll remember forever: the day you lost your cool, or said something you wish you hadn't, or didn't speak up when you should have.

Before we begin to pick apart practices that you, reader, may have used or may still be using in the classroom, it's important to stress that we know how hard teaching is, and we know the special regret teachers feel when they think they have fallen short of the duty they owe to their students. This is not a book of chastisement or a book to be used as ammunition or for self-flagellation. We are not writing it to be critical of what you or your colleagues do.

If being perfect is the qualification for writing this book, we are certainly not qualified; many of the revelations you will read about were sparked by incidents in our own classrooms. But if learning from mistakes qualifies us to write this book, then we certainly hit the mark. Our goal was to write a book that we wish had existed when we were starting out as teachers. With that in mind, we have focused on explaining the problems associated with 16 established classroom practices. After we present the problems associated with these practices, we present better, easy-to-implement alternatives that meet the same, or similar, goals those practices are intended to achieve. Here are the 16 problematic practices we address:

- Round robin reading
- Teaching to learning styles
- Homework as the default
- Using interim assessments as "formative assessments"
- Asking, "Does everybody understand?"
- Traditional Q&A
- Data-driven everything
- Publicly displayed data walls
- Content breadth over depth
- Adhering to rigid pacing guides
- Teaching to the test samplers
- An analysis-only approach to reading
- Shortchanging science and social studies
- Ignoring curriculum experts
- Using behavior charts
- Withholding recess

The Limitations of Research and the Rewards of Reflection

Although you will encounter research findings that support opposition to current persistent practices that "feel right" but actually undermine student learning, in some cases there is little direct data proving that something is a bad practice. Remember, much of what is studied in the field of education needs to be approved by a panel of reviewers whose sole purpose is to ensure high ethical standards. These academic research ethics committees ensure that participants are protected and that the research will not place subjects in positions of peril or risk. For example, universities have institutional review boards (IRBs) that must approve studies prior to the research being conducted. If they are doing their jobs, these review boards will prohibit a study from taking place if it seems likely to place children in the position of being the recipients of questionable practices. This is why you won't find studies that compare an experimental group subjected to a commonly agreed-upon "bad teaching practice" with a group that received "effective teaching." There are ethical boundaries that limit the type of research that can be conducted with students. That's a good thing, but it also presents challenges that can perpetuate ineffective and potentially harmful habits in K–12 classrooms that continue without clear and recent opposition.

We encourage you to talk about the topics in this book with trusted teacher friends, reflect on them together, and evaluate what is and is not working with your own students. We admit that we don't have every answer. You don't have to agree with every conclusion we come to, but please weigh the benefits against the costs when considering your own teaching practices. And, when appropriate, ask your students for input, using some of the simple student surveys included in this book. Students usually know what works and what doesn't; after all, they are living it. Give them opportunities to tell you. Listen to what they have to say.

Our Intended Audience

This book is for teachers at all stages—novices, veterans, and everyone in between—as well as for teacher-prep candidates who will raise the next generation of world-changers. But most important, this book is for the children most affected by these practices.

Teachers, there are better ways. Let's use them, for the sake of our students and for our own peace of mind.

1
Round Robin Reading

> **You've gotta ask yourself one question: "Do I feel lucky?"**
> *Dirty Harry*, 1971

Imagine that you are a developing or struggling reader sitting in a classroom, surrounded by more proficient readers. Like many days, today's agenda calls for a round robin reading of a piece of text—material that you're encountering for the very first time.

To mix things up, today the teacher is using "popcorn reading," a variation of round robin in which she randomly calls on students to read. This twist is meant to keep you focused; unlike regular round robin, you can't count the paragraphs and the number of students in your row, identify which piece you'll be reading, and practice it in your mind ahead of time. You're supposed to just listen, absorb, and be ready. So there you are, a developing reader who struggles with fluency, waiting to have the spotlight turned on you. How are you feeling? How do you think you'll do? Will you be lucky and get words that are familiar—the ones that you know how to pronounce? Will you sound confident? Will you look "stupid"?

The teacher calls your name. *You're up.* Your best friend sitting next to you graciously points to the passage that you're supposed to read. You begin haltingly, and soon a couple of students are jumping in to "help" you any time you stumble. The teacher strolls the rows of desks, interrupting to correct a word or two as you read. She means well and is focused on providing support and making notes to herself, but you're only thinking about one thing: judgment. "OK, thank you," she says, and calls on the next reader.

You did it. What are you thinking about? Are you thinking about the content of the text you just read or that your successor is currently reading? And how are you feeling? Proud? Humiliated? More important, how are you feeling, right now, about the overall act of reading?

Though it felt like an eternity, your reading lasted less than one minute. You read a total of 37 words during the 28 minutes your class spent on this round robin reading activity. Although the instructional intent was to build your fluency and comprehension, we're going to argue that not only did this round robin reading experience do little to help you become a better reader, it may actually have hindered your literacy progress and put an additional barrier between you and the content. Round robin reading is ineffective on multiple counts, including that it can feel like a pointless slog. But its greatest indictment is that, for the most vulnerable students, it is far from being harmless.

What's Problematic About Round Robin Reading?

Round robin's specific forms vary, but it always involves the teacher calling on students to read out loud, one by one, in front of their peers.

Much of why teachers use round robin boils down to their desire to have more control over the learning. If only one student is reading at a time, the teacher can focus completely on that one student. Middle and high school teachers will sometimes require round robin reading in order to be certain that students have actually read the text and be able to jump in and ensure comprehension of the text. But more often than not, the opposite of what is intended occurs. Fluency suffers, comprehension suffers, and students do not typically follow along with the text being read (Fair & Combs, 2011).

It is safe to say that if reading held a party, round robin would not be invited. Few teaching practices have been so maligned by experts yet embraced by teachers as much as this longtime staple of American classrooms. We earned our first graduate degrees about three decades ago, and even then, the limited research on this strategy suggested that it was ineffective in promoting literacy. Our university professors flat-out warned us it could sabotage the rest of our reading instruction. And yet, we have seen round robin reading practiced consistently and widely over the past 30 years. In a 2009 study, Ash and colleagues found that over half of K–8 teachers in U.S. schools self-reported using round robin reading as an instructional practice. We have found in our own research that the strategy still enjoys a prominent place in classrooms (Himmele et al., 2021). We still see it in our own visits to schools—as recently as yesterday.

Indeed, despite round robin's continued popularity, it is very much a pariah among literacy experts. Richard Allington, former president of the International Literacy Association and prolific literacy author, writes that the strategy fosters "interruptive behavior, and under those conditions, readers begin to read more slowly and tentatively" (Allington, 2013, p. 527). "Studies suggest that much of the time devoted to round robin reading is wasted in terms of student learning," notes Timothy Shanahan, former president of the International Literacy Association and one of the lead writers for the National Reading Panel (Shanahan, 2005, p. 18). Literacy expert Michael Opitz and reading fluency expert Timothy Rasinski write that "although oral reading can be beneficial, round robin reading is not. It more often prohibits rather than facilitates the ability to read" (Opitz & Rasinski, 2008, p. 12). Reading Hall of Fame inductee D. Ray Reutzel and prolific reading expert Robert Cooter Jr. (2019) offer a clear verdict: "Our advice? Never use round robin in your classroom" (p. 201).

Among the first researchers to question the validity of round robin reading was Dolores Durkin. In the 1970s, Durkin studied the use of this strategy in 3rd through 6th grade social studies lessons, finding that teachers spent between 8 and 10 percent of these lessons in round robin reading with little to no focus on comprehension. Her research confirmed that round robin reading was not enough to help students successfully read social studies textbooks. "[N]o teacher saw the social studies period as a time to help with reading," she wrote. "Children who could not read the textbook were expected to learn the content from round robin reading of the text by better readers, and from films and filmstrips" (Durkin, 1978–79, p. 502).

By the mid-1990s, round robin reading was being referred to as "outmoded" (Harris & Hodges, 1995) despite remaining very much present in everyday practice.

Putting Round Robin to the Test

Because there are so few studies directly addressing the effectiveness of round robin reading, we decided to conduct a little research of our own by subjecting 115 senior-level undergraduates in five different teacher education courses to a round robin reading activity—with a twist: to prevent unintentionally embarrassing anyone, we secretly preselected 20 students to call upon and allowed them to practice reading the text beforehand. And even though we were working with college-age students, we had to agree to numerous risk-reduction factors before receiving approval to conduct this activity (Himmele et al., 2021). Afterward, we asked all students to complete anonymous surveys describing the experience and explaining any memories of round robin reading in the classroom that the exercise brought up. Here are a few of the themes that emerged, along with illustrative statements from the students:

- **Attempts to count ahead:** "The strongest memory is in 10th grade ancient mythology, when we read *The Odyssey*. I remember counting people and trying to figure out what paragraph I would have to read."
- **Feeling like a "bad reader":** "My most vivid memory is from 7th grade English. I wasn't a great reader, so I would get hung up on words in front of everyone, and the teacher would wait a few seconds to help."
- **Bullying, embarrassment, or loss of status:** "One kid in my class would struggle a lot, take a while to read, and then after a while some kids in my class would grunt when he got called on—they'd be like, 'Ughhhh'—and he already wouldn't want to read."
- **Emotional stress that manifests physically:** "The anxiety I was feeling caused my brain to shut down. I felt worried that I wouldn't be able to pronounce any of the words. I started to sweat, higher heart rate, increased breathing."
- **Anxiety-induced confusion:** "I would get so stressed that I would not even comprehend any material. I was so worried about

messing up. I would try to figure out what paragraph I had to read and practice it in my head."

We strongly believe that one of the quickest ways to make students hate the act of reading is to subject them to this barrage of negative emotions when they try to read.

Academic Drawbacks

One of the main criticisms of round robin reading is that it is inefficient, with students spending most of their time waiting and getting very little time to actually read. "Let's face it," writes Shanahan (2019), "in a 30-minute social studies lesson [using round robin reading], each kid would typically get to read a minute or less. That means social studies would add fewer than three hours of reading time per year—not enough to help the kids" (para. 32). The problem extends to working with small groups. Allington (2013) notes how much more efficient silent reading is than round robin reading: "In silent reading activity, everyone is engaged in reading, so during the same period of time, children engaged in silent reading read three to five times as much text as during a round robin reading event" (pp. 526–527).

In addition to being inefficient, round robin reading does not appear to support comprehension (Durkin, 1978–79; Eldredge et al., 1996). As Durkin (1981) observed in her study of the strategy, "Even though able students followed along, it was often ineffective. They stumbled over hard-to-pronounce words, read in a monotone, and were difficult to hear" (p. 454). This lack of fluency makes comprehension a challenge, and it's one reason Shanahan (2014) notes that "a reading comprehension lesson, except with the youngest children, should emphasize silent reading—and lots of it" (p. 187).

"Active interactive strategic processes are critically necessary to the development of reading comprehension," writes the National Reading Panel (2000, p. 41); these "active interactive strategic processes" are absent during round robin reading. There is a schedule to be maintained, and before a student has time to even process what they read aloud (assuming they were focusing on meaning), the next student is called upon to read.

Indeed, round robin reading "actively damages learners' comprehension of text and delays their fluency development" (Ash et al., 2009, p. 88).

For the round robin activity we conducted with our students, we chose to read a selection from Paulo Freire's *Pedagogy of the Oppressed*. The selection was complex, but we had introduced it in an assigned reading that touched on the concept of "listening objects." Following the exercise, when asked if they comprehended what they read, a full 74 percent of students reported that they hadn't. One student said, "I didn't remember or comprehend anything that was read because I was scanning for unknown words in case I was the next victim." This was a common theme. Another student shared, "I couldn't tell you what I read or was being read. I was just so focused on following along to be ready to read when I was called on." By contrast, only 20 percent of students reported they somewhat understood what was read. As one student said, "I feel like I understood most of what was being read, but I was worried that I was going to get called on, so I wasn't fully paying attention." Only five students (approximately 5 percent) said they understood what was read (Himmele et al., 2021).

Reading proficiency is complex. Consider the concepts of "automaticity" and "prosody." Automaticity refers to the effortless and accurate reading of words (LaBerge & Samuels, 1974), and prosody refers to the intonation, rhythm, and expression with which readers read. Together, automaticity and prosody combine to create reading fluency, one of the essential foundational skills for reading (Rasinski, 2012). Both skills also support (and are indicators of) reading comprehension (National Reading Panel, 2000; Reutzel & Cooter, 2019; Shanahan, 2015). Under No Child Left Behind (NCLB), the skill of fluency was often measured using timed tests to record percentile ranks based on accuracy and reading speed. A child who flew past punctuation and barreled through sentences, reading without expression (indicative of a lack of comprehension), might thus be deemed fluent using such tests, which failed to take prosody into consideration. Partly due to this skewed emphasis on certain components of fluency (i.e., automaticity over prosody), many teachers have come to wrongly equate fluency with reading speed (Rasinski, 2011).

True reading fluency will always be an essential foundational skill for readers. "Less fluent readers struggle through text in a labored word-by-word manner," note Reutzel and Cooter (2019). "They focus most of their attention on decoding or figuring out how to pronounce words, so reading comprehension suffers" (p. 179). As Rasinski and Padak (2013) put it, if readers "have to use too much . . . cognitive energy to decode the words in text, they have little remaining for the more important task in reading—comprehension. These students are marked by their slow, laborious, staccato reading of texts" (pp. 2–3). Although oral reading usually supports fluency, Allington (2013) argues that round robin reading seems to have the opposite effect: "The interruptive round robin oral reading lesson fosters the dysfluency that typically marks the oral reading behaviors of struggling readers" (p. 527).

Emotional Drawbacks

For many students, adolescence is a time of heightened self-awareness. Most of us remember those socially awkward middle school years when we felt as though all eyes were on us, when even the slightest embarrassment suffered resulted in deep humiliation.

We recently spoke with an accomplished special education administrator who was close to retirement. He recounted one awful day during his middle school years when his teacher was using round robin reading, and he counted ahead to practice the paragraph that he would be assigned. As a socially awkward kid and a struggling reader, his hope was to minimize the shame of "performing" before an audience of unforgiving peers. What he hadn't counted on was that the student ahead of him would falter, and the teacher would assign him the task of finishing the section he hadn't known to practice. Panic descended. What would have normally, for him, been a halting attempt to read was now punctuated by overwhelming fear, and his performance showed it. "I'll never forget that day," he told us, 50 years later. He described it as one of the worst days in his schooling career. "I absolutely hate round robin reading," he told us. "Please tell teachers that it's past time to put that practice to rest."

There's no doubt about it: round robin reading can be profoundly humiliating to students, and especially to self-conscious adolescents. "Unfortunately, this approach only further alienates struggling readers and removes them from the learning experience," write Fair and Combs

(2011). "These children will 'leave' the classroom, mentally, emotionally, and in some cases physically" (p. 226). Students who struggle with reading have little experience with the joys it can bring, meaning they lack the best incentive there is to keep trying and, thus, to become better at it.

The stress students experience during round robin reading serves to turn them off not just from reading but from deeper learning. As child trauma expert Bruce Perry said in a 2004 lecture, "Children in a state of fear retrieve information from the world differently than children who feel calm. In a state of calm, we use the higher, more complex parts of our brain to process and act on information. In a state of fear, we use the lower, more primitive parts of our brain. As the perceived threat level goes up, the less thoughtful and the more reactive our responses become. Actions in this state may be governed by emotional and reactive thinking styles." Kelleher and Whitman (2020) also note that emotion and cognition are intertwined: "When students experience trauma, toxic stress, or even episodic stress, the fight, flight, or freeze response makes learning difficult to impossible" (para. 6).

Stephanie Jones (2013) describes the trauma that a round robin reading activity reawakened in her college students: "Students report sweating, feeling hot, noticing their heart rate speed up, shaking legs, and fearing humiliation and being perceived as incompetent. . . . Few reported being able to understand the printed text on which the activity was supposed to be focused. I—and the discursive practice—successfully produced failure in the task at hand (if the goal, indeed, is to make sense of the printed text)" (p. 527).

Michael Opitz also immersed his college students in a round robin reading activity, and his students also reported physical signs of stress: "'My hands were sweating.'. . . 'My heart started to race, and I had trouble breathing.' . . . Some talk[ed] about how they actually got sick to their stomachs in anticipation of their turn, others about how their hands and voices would tremble uncontrollably" (Opitz & Rasinski, 2008, p. xvii). Remember, these were college students, with presumably college-level literacy skills. Imagine how much worse the effect is bound to be on younger readers or on anyone who is still developing fluency.

Positive Alternatives to Round Robin Reading

Extensive oral reading practice improves fluency, which in turn improves reading comprehension: "With primary grade readers (grade 2), about 70 percent of the variation in reading comprehension is due to variance in fluency" (Shanahan, 2015, para. 5). But as we've discussed, round robin reading actually provides each individual student with very little practice. It subjects them to anxiety and can even lead to long-lasting negative feelings toward reading. Here, then, are some healthy alternatives to round robin. Some strategies provide better ways to engage students in the kind of oral reading practice that supports fluency, and others are practices that support comprehension and deeper processing of the texts that students read.

Strategies for the Primary Grades

We know oral reading is important for developing fluency, and fluency affects comprehension. But how do you get students to read orally (so you can attend to fluency) without round robin reading? Our answer to that is simple: *read together*. Alternative options for practicing reading aloud include choral reading, shared reading, and singing lyrics while looking at the words, pointing to the words, and reading the words aloud. Additionally, using individual reading conferences to monitor students' progress in reading is an essential component of adequately assessing each student's strengths and needs.

Choral reading

Choral reading provides a low-risk opportunity for students to practice reading text out loud at the same time. Because students all read at the same time, they are all engaged in practice throughout the length of the exercise. "For those students who may be a bit reticent to perform on their own or may have some difficulty in reading, the support from the entire group of readers allows all readers to be successful" (Opitz & Rasinski, 2008, p. 51).

Start by modeling the reading while students use their fingers to track the words. Next, reread the text aloud along with students as they again use their fingers to track. You should be able to see fingers on the words and students mouthing the words while they read them. It can help to pause at the beginning of the page and lead a countdown to a common start: "One, two, ready, begin. . . ."

This exercise works best with young or struggling readers who have not yet developed enough skill to read silently without assistance. Although David Paige (2011) provides evidence that choral reading can also help intermediate-age readers who struggle with reading, we would encourage teachers to evaluate its appropriateness with students who are already able to silently read on their own. If students can read on their own, choral reading may not be the best choice for them, unless they are struggling with fluency development.

Shared reading

In 1996, Eldredge and colleagues published one of the few experimental studies in existence comparing the use of round robin reading with another approach—in this case, the Shared Book Experience (which we refer to here as the "shared reading approach" or just "shared reading," since the texts do not need to be books).

In this strategy, students and teachers "read enlarged versions of books [aloud and together], and while the stories are read, teachers touch the words of the enlarged text so children can match written and spoken words. Initially the teacher does most of the reading, but as the children become familiar with the text, they join in and 'share' the reading" (Eldredge et al., 1996, p. 202). The researchers found that when compared to round robin reading, shared reading produced greater achievement gains "on all measures of reading growth: vocabulary acquisition, word analysis, word recognition, reading fluency, and reading comprehension" (p. 218). And it has a simple numerical advantage over round robin reading: instead of only reading a small, assigned portion of a text, students might be exposed to hundreds of words. Because they read chorally, they don't need to dread reading alone.

Shared reading usually is most appropriate for young learners in kindergarten through 2nd grade. As in choral reading, this strategy typically begins with the teacher modeling the reading of a text, followed by all students reading the text out loud at the same time. Shared reading can be a whole-class or small-group experience, as long as everyone shares a single text and the reading strategies used are introduced via this one text.

When conducting a shared reading, make sure students are looking at the words and "open-mouth reading" (as opposed to silent, closed-mouth reading) along with you as you use a pointer to point to the written words. You may need to remind students, but they should be looking at the words as they say them—otherwise they're not really practicing reading. Again, we know that this may seem obvious, but if students are not actually looking at the words, they are not reading. We repeat this here, because we have observed ineffective shared reading lessons where students were mumbling along but not actually looking at the words. It's easy for students to memorize a poem, text, or song, but if you really want to make sure they are reading, ask them to look at the words or, if the words are in front of them, to drag a finger under the words as they read. Figure 1.1 (see pp. 18–19) presents ideas for developing a variety of literacy skills using shared reading.

Here are some tips for ensuring that shared reading proves successful in your classroom:

- Select a song, big book, or poem to focus on for the week or for however many days is appropriate. Make sure it is written in large enough text for all students to see while they are seated in a designated reading area.
- For some of the activities, students will need individual copies of the text to track with their fingers. Consider introducing the individual student copies on the second or third day so that the students will have already watched you model and track the words on the large, shared reading text.
- Dedicate a 20- to 30-minute portion of the morning to shared reading time, but feel free to also sprinkle in extra time during the day whenever you have a few minutes free.
- Be strategic in choosing the skills to focus on. The skills listed in Figure 1.1 are not meant to be taught all in one day. They are meant to be selected as needed, and they can be revisited every subsequent week. A few skills can be revisited daily; for example, students in Pérsida's class used to chorally read every day and spend time daily pointing to words and stretching and blending letter sounds.

Figure 1.1—Shared Reading Strategies by Skill Category

Comprehension and Story Elements

1. Introduce the cover and make predictions about the story.
2. Point to the words as you model reading the story with expression.
3. Ask comprehension questions and have students pair-share answers. Ask about story elements like settings, characters, problem.
4. Ask students to join in with repetitive patterns.
5. Ask students to provide text-based evidence in response to "How do you know?" types of questions: "Point to the part in the story that made you think that; now share it with a partner."
6. Make inferences: "What do we know about the character? What was he/she feeling? What in the book makes you think that? Share your reasons with a partner."

Fluency, Vocabulary, and Word Choice

1. After modeling the reading, chorally read the enlarged text together. Choral reading will be the most important component of shared reading, in terms of building fluency, so do this part every day, making sure that students' eyes are on the words.
2. Give students a printout of the whole text. Ask students to drag a finger under each word of the printout as it is being read out loud together. Read it several times. Use a large font so that you can monitor that students' fingers are on the right word.
3. Identify and focus on high-frequency words using highlighter tape.
4. Point to key words. Ask students to slowly and silently mouth the sounds as you slowly glide across each letter of the word.
5. Ask students to show you what the words mean using body movements.
6. Highlight the author's selection of specific words. What effect do these words have? What other words would have worked?

Conventions and Previously Introduced Skills

1. Read the story, pointing out capital letters and stopping at periods, exclamation points, and other punctuation marks.
2. Focus on syntax. Place sticky notes on certain words (e.g., the verbs or describing words/adjectives). Ask, "What other describing words could fit? How might we spell that word?" Prompt students to "write" the word on the carpet, using their finger. Write the new word on a sticky note. Address parts of speech for these words.
3. Model making inferences and reading strategies that strategic readers use when faced with a challenge.
4. Revisit and focus on features of literacy or language that have been recently introduced.

Phonemic Awareness, Phonics, and Stretching Words

1. Chorally read the text.
2. S T R E T C H the word. Sound the word out grapheme by grapheme. Slowly drag your pointer across the word as the students sound out each part by silently mouthing the sounds as you point to them, and then audibly chorally making the sounds as you point to them—thus stretching and blending the word (select words that can be sounded out).
3. Focus on the rhyming words. Predict rhyming words that are covered with sticky notes. Prompt students to tell you other words that might have fit.

Slowly lift the sticky note, uncovering one letter at a time, sounding out each grapheme as you go: "Silently mouth each sound as I uncover it. Show me with your mouth, but don't say it out loud, yet . . . and 1, 2, 3, shout it out!"

4. Focus on phonics by pointing out the matching letters in the rhyming words.
5. Separate the phonemes. "What are the sounds you hear in the word *mat?*" Ask all students to silently mouth each of the sounds that you hear. "Now, go ahead and write the sound on the carpet, using your finger, as we say it."
6. Use highlighter tape to focus on and point out consonant blends (*bl, st, dr*), digraphs (*ch, sh, th*), dipthongs (*ou, oi, oy*), or other phonic elements in the words. Have students mouth the sounds when you point to them.
7. Find the word ____. Point to and mouth the word. "Why do you think it says _____ and not ____ (choose a visually similar word)? Explain it to your neighbor."
8. Replace blends with other letters or blends to make new words.
9. Examine matching letters in rhyming patterns.

Awareness of Story Structure and Author's Voice

1. Select favorite parts of the story to celebrate.
2. Compare works with other previously read works created by the same author or other authors.
3. Create and illustrate a sequential retelling of the story.
4. Role-play the story in small groups.
5. Artistically present the story with some or all of the text included within the final product.
6. Illustrate individual student books.
7. Modify or personalize the story by replacing key words with personalized words.
8. Create a class book (with students illustrating one page for each individual or pair).
9. Write a found poem using the interesting words collected on a book-specific word wall. (Found poems are random words selected from the story and arranged in a list, or in an artistic way.)

- Limit your talk. Be strategic about how much time children spend in "open-mouth reading" during your shared reading time. This is how you build fluency in a fun and communal way. The more you talk, the less time students will spend reading.

Song lyric study

As a 1st grade teacher, Pérsida regularly made use of songs and song lyrics to help teach her students to read. Other than making sure the songs were upbeat and contained no mature content, she spent little time selecting them. Some weren't even technically children's songs, and they included words that were more difficult than those her 6- and 7-year-olds might be able to read independently. For example, one of the students' favorite songs to read was Louis Armstrong's "What a Wonderful World." (Pérsida "borrowed" the idea of using this song-based big book from a classroom she visited, and it quickly became a staple in her primary classrooms.) Though clearly not written at the typical 1st grade reading level, this song allowed students to be exposed to reading in a fun and communal way. As the song played, they followed the lyrics with their fingers. They also searched for and stretched key words, and manipulated the text according to Pérsida's instructions.

For two years straight, Pérsida's class consisted mainly of English learners, all of whom left 1st grade as readers of English—all of them. Though her literacy instruction included targeted exposure to practice decoding and reading text, Pérsida credits her students' reading growth to the volume of comprehensible print that each student read aloud every single day, much of it in the form of song lyrics. She followed a standard format, included here, that featured multiple exposures to a particular song throughout the week. Each daily exposure to the "song of the week" lasted for approximately 20 to 30 minutes, including singing and reviewing former songs selected by the students. (At our website, TotalParticipation Techniques.com, you can see a video where Pérsida shares an actual copy of a student-made big book featuring the song of the week, along with a list of songs that might work in your classroom.)

Here are the steps you can take each day to embed music in your daily shared reading schedule:

- **Day 1.** Start the week by introducing a new song. Write its lyrics on a piece of chart paper, then hang the paper from the ceiling or in a new spot around the classroom. Every week, the students will start looking for the new song, and you'll hear an excited little buzz as they try to decipher the lyrics on their own. When it's time to read, ask your students to come down to your reading circle area. You'll want them close, both so that they can all see the text and so that you can make sure they are tracking the words. Introduce the song and hit play on whatever device you're using, letting the students listen to the song as you grab a pointer and point to the words on the chart paper as each is sung. Comment on any interesting or fun words. Next, ask the students to sing the song while keeping their eyes on the words to which you are pointing. Tell them that doing this will help them become "smooth readers." Be sure to monitor their reading and remind them why they should keep their eyes on the words. Keep older songs displayed for weeks at a time, so that students can revisit them and practice using the pointer to sing and read them during their free time.

- **Day 2.** Pass out one copy of the lyrics to the song for each child. You'll want the text to be large enough (about 18 to 20 points) so that you can see what words students point to from wherever you stand in the reading circle. Read the lyrics from the large sheet you used on Day 1, monitoring as the students read along from their sheets. Let students know that if they lose track, they should look around and see where their peers are pointing. Let them know that there is no shame in losing their place.
- **Day 3.** Play "find that word" (e.g., "On line 2, there is a word that has the *br* sound. Find it and point to it, then mouth it for me"). Stretch the words as you read or sing. As you drag your pointer ever so slowly over a word (choose one that is easily decodable), ask the students to sound out the parts. Continue repeatedly singing the song and pointing to the words as each is read.
- **Day 4.** Take an extra lyric sheet and cut out each numbered line, handing one line apiece to each student or pair of students. Give students a large sheet of construction paper and ask them to copy the line in a large enough print for students in the back of the reading circle to see. (The first few times, you'll likely need to walk around the room and make sure that the text they are copying is large enough; Pérsida's students tended to write in teeny-tiny letters.) If necessary, trace what the students have written with a fine-point black marker for extra visibility. When everyone is finished, compile all the pages into the weekly classroom big book.
- **Day 5.** Read and sing from the classroom big book, then ceremonially place it in your classroom library for students to borrow during their independent reading times.

Strategies for Intermediate and Secondary Grades

The following alternatives to round robin reading address the literacy needs of adolescent readers—namely, fluency support, motivation, and comprehension. None of these ideas are new; in fact, you'll likely notice some that have been around for decades.

Multisensory fluency support

Although Pérsida used songs in the primary grades, there is evidence that singing while reading lyrics improves reading even among struggling middle school students. One study by Biggs and colleagues (2008) found that students who did this experienced an average of seven months of reading growth over the study's nine-week period! Likewise, choral reading can help some older students who struggle with reading. Sixteen minutes of daily choral reading were found by Paige (2011) to help intermediate-aged readers develop decoding and fluency skills.

Oral assisted reading, also known as the neurological impress method (NIM), is another practice proven to increase the fluency and comprehension of adolescent readers (Flood et al., 2005; Hollingsworth, 1978; Young et al., 2018). Heckelman (1969) found that children with reading disabilities who experienced up to seven hours of NIM showed an average of two grade levels of growth in oral reading ability. NIM is similar to choral reading, in that it involves more than one reader reading the same text at the same time. While variations exist, the gist is simple: a more advanced reader, teacher, or tutor sits in such a way that the student can clearly hear them reading. The student then reads aloud alongside the tutor, while tracking the words with their fingers. Rasinski (2011) describes NIM in this way: "a neurological trace of the sight and sound of the words in the text would be laid out in the mind of the struggling reader that was similar to the trace that existed in the mind of the more advanced reader" (p. 241).

All of these practices have one thing in common: *they are multisensory approaches to reading*. Students are hearing the words while also seeing them and saying them out loud. These practices may be particularly helpful for English learners (ELs) who must learn to read, listen, and speak in their new language.

Reading choice and engagement

The more students read, the better readers they become (Krashen, 2004). Unfortunately, poor readers spend significantly more time *learning about how to read* than they do actually reading (Gambrell et al., 2001), which limits their access to the best and most motivating part of reading: the worlds it opens to readers.

Linda Gambrell (2011) highlights seven classroom practices proven to increase students' reading motivation and achievement:

1. Access to a range of reading materials
2. Opportunities for students to choose what they read
3. Adequate time for students to engage in sustained reading
4. Opportunities for success with challenging texts
5. Opportunities for social interactions about text
6. Opportunities to engage in reading tasks that have relevance
7. Incentives that reflect the value of reading and learning (not stickers or candy, but things like effective, pointed, and specific teacher commendations and feedback, free books, or book-related incentives)

Repeated readings also build fluency, but note that students aren't likely to become motivated readers by repeatedly reading the same text, day in and day out. Provide plenty of opportunities for building silent reading fluency through self-selected texts as well. Additionally, Allington (2009) cautions that "repeated readings as an instructional strategy ought to be used with moderation because it limits the total number of new words that children will read, and the total number of words children read is an important component of fluency development" (p. 25).

Reciprocal reading

Reciprocal reading is a collaborative reading technique that supports comprehension as well as each student's ability to monitor their own growth in comprehension (Hattie, 2009; Palincsar & Brown, 1984). The technique allows for teachers to model how to actively make meaning of the text by questioning, summarizing, clarifying, and predicting.

Select three or four students to model this technique in class by working in groups with one student designated as the first "teacher." Give each group a reading selection that contains stopping points where the role of "teacher" can transfer to another student. Providing students with a bookmark, like the one in Figure 1.2, can help them remember their roles and tasks (Palincsar & Brown, 1984).

Figure 1.2—Reciprocal "Teacher" Bookmark

Your Role as a Reciprocal Teacher

1. Read
Everyone silently reads the section.

2. Ask a question
Find the main idea and create a question that addresses the main idea. Ask the students in your group the question.

3. Summarize the paragraph
Share your summary with the students. Ask them to let you know if you missed anything.

4. Clarify
Check to see if everyone understands or if anyone has any questions.

5. Make predictions
What do your group members think the next sections will be about? Ask them to tell you why they predict this.

Now it's the next "teacher's" turn to do the same.

Conclusion

Though the problems associated with round robin reading have been known for decades, the practice remains widespread in classrooms. The good news is that there are better ways to monitor student learning, build fluency, and promote reading comprehension.

Figure 1.3 presents a survey that teachers can use to get feedback from their students about round robin reading. You'll want to explain to students what "round robin reading" means. If you decide that the surveys should be anonymous, explain that to students. If not, then be sure to explain that no one will be penalized for sharing their honest opinions. Don't be surprised if the stronger readers actually enjoy the strategy. For them, it is an opportunity to showcase their strengths. Pay special attention to responses from those who struggle: for them, round robin reading is not just ineffective but can also be harmful.

Figure 1.3—Student Survey: Round Robin Reading

1. I enjoy round robin reading (when people take turns reading out loud in class).

5–strongly agree 4–agree 3–no opinion 2–disagree 1–strongly disagree

Please elaborate:

2. I feel like I do a very good job reading aloud during round robin reading.

5–strongly agree 4–agree 3–no opinion 2–disagree 1–strongly disagree

Please elaborate:

3. I feel nervous about reading out loud when my name is called.

5–strongly agree 4–agree 3–no opinion 2–disagree 1–strongly disagree

Please elaborate:

4. When it is other students' time to read out loud, I listen carefully to what they read.

5–strongly agree 4–agree 3–no opinion 2–disagree 1–strongly disagree

Please elaborate:

5. When teachers use round robin reading, I feel like I am really learning.

5–strongly agree 4–agree 3–no opinion 2–disagree 1–strongly disagree

Please elaborate:

2

Teaching to Learning Styles

I'll be back.
The Terminator, 1984

We have a friend who has eight children. If you ask him how many children he has, he'll say, "I have eight kids—one of each." He's onto something. Every child is different, even those who are raised in the same household.

So if all children are different, does that mean they also all learn differently? And if they do, is there a way to categorize those differences so that we can strategically meet each child's needs in the classroom? Enter learning style theory. It sounds so good—so personalized, so student-focused. Trouble is, there's little evidence that teaching to "learning styles" actually *works*. And, while teaching to learning styles may not be hugely detrimental to students, it can distract us from the fact that there are better, more strategic ways to view learners and how they interact with the content.

What's Problematic About Teaching to Learning Styles?

Learning style theory holds that every student learns best when content is presented in a way that targets that student's individual way of learning. Thousands of articles and dozens of books address learning styles, identifying at least 70 different variations and modalities (Pashler et al., 2008).

The ones that really seem to have taken root in teachers' minds are those of visual, auditory, and kinesthetic learning styles, which has led to classification of students as *visual learners, auditory learners,* and *kinesthetic learners* (Barbe et al., 1979; Dunn et al., 1984; Fleming & Mills, 1992). The decades-old idea posits that students have a preferred way of processing information, and they can do so more effectively when that information is delivered in a way that aligns with their preference.

There are at least three major problems associated with these theories.

First, teaching to specific learning styles can mean presenting content in ways that are not actually optimal for learning that content, rendering lessons less effective rather than more. For example, some content, by its very nature, is better presented visually. A teacher would more effectively show students landforms rather than solely explaining them. An even more effective presentation would also involve students drawing them in their notes and creating hand gestures to symbolize their meanings.

Second, if students are made aware of the learning style that someone has identified them as having, they may internalize the belief that they can only learn when content is presented in that particular learning style. Students start to believe they can only learn well in one specific way, and self-perceived weaknesses can become self-fulfilling prophecies (Dweck, 2006). For example, if I believe I am a visual learner and not an auditory one, I may decide there's no point working on my listening skills because "that's not how I learn." We see this in our university setting when advisees explain to us that they want to drop a course because the professor's presentation style conflicts with their learning style. What strategies have they explored for mastering the content they are finding so challenging? None that they can articlate; their assumptions have led them to believe that there wasn't any point in trying.

The third and rightfully most significant problem with learning style theory is that the research fails to support that teaching to learning styles actually works (Cook et al., 2009; Hattie & Yates, 2014). In the words of Rohrer and Pashler (2012), "There exist a smattering of positive findings with unknown effect sizes that are eclipsed by a much greater number of published failures" (p. 634).

Analyses of various studies show that instruction aimed at learning styles does not improve learning (Kavale & Forness, 1987; Rohrer & Pashler, 2012; Willingham, 2015). "Research from the last 10 years confirms that matching instruction to learning style brings no benefit," writes Willingham (2018). "But other research points to a new conclusion: people do have biases about preferred modes of thinking, even though these biases don't help them think better." Meanwhile, teaching in a way that suits the content has been shown to be more effective than teaching toward a particular learning style. As Willingham (2005) puts it, "What does matter is whether the child is taught in the content's best modality. All students learn more when content drives the choice of modality." Although students may differ in their learning preferences, their preferred way of learning may not be the most effective.

Despite these facts, learning style theories continue to thrive in our classrooms (Boser, 2019; Macdonald et al., 2017). "The contrast between the enormous popularity of the learning styles approach within education and the lack of credible evidence for its utility is, in our opinion, striking and disturbing," write Pashler and colleagues (2008). "If classification of students' learning styles has practical utility, it remains to be demonstrated" (p. 117). According to Hattie and Yates (2014), "there is not any recognized evidence suggesting that knowing or diagnosing learning styles will help you to teach your students any better than not knowing their learning styles. And we certainly want to be clear: learning styles are not the same as developing various learning strategies" (p. 176).

The Learning Styles "Neuromyth"

But like the Terminator's famous pronouncement—"I'll be back"—educators can be assured that new references to learning styles will continue to pop up, even among highly respected sources.

What causes learning style theories to have such staying power despite the lack of proof of efficacy? The internet is full of websites suggesting ways to teach to different learning styles, especially ones focused on students with special needs. Boser (2019) surveyed more than 200 educators and found that 97 percent of respondents endorsed the enduring "neuromyth" of teaching to learning styles. Even state certification gatekeepers appear to believe in the practice: Furey (2020) found that state-issued teacher-certification exam prep materials in 29 states still contained information about learning styles. We found that some university teacher education websites and required course textbooks also endorse learning style theory (as these websites may not reflect the views of all faculty, we will not name the schools here). Such messages from trusted sources go a long way toward explaining why the myths remain so hard to dispel.

Ojure and Sherman (2001) also suggest some practical reasons why teachers may be drawn to learning styles: "Teachers intuitively perceive that students differ in how they learn," they note, "and that those differences are important to understand" (p. 33). The teachers whom Ojure and Sherman studied believed that workshops devoted to learning styles made a positive difference in their practice, even though they did not adopt all of the beliefs and practices the workshops suggested. And perhaps the workshops *did* provide teachers with practical strategies for presenting information in effective ways that capture student attention. But we would be limiting the ability of students to deeply learn something if we used the same modality at all times with any given student. Our goal is to help students to deeply understand and to store meaning, not just to memorize sounds and visuals and kinesthetic actions. As Willingham (2018) writes, "Data show that people do have some propensity to use one or another mode of thinking, but people would be better off if they didn't; rather, they should use the mode of thinking that's a better fit for the task at hand" (para. 24).

The Appeal to Teachers

Another big reason learning styles have stuck around so long is that so many teachers just love the idea. Some dismiss the arguments debunking learning style theory even before hearing them. Many were drawn to learning styles based on their understanding that children are each unique in their own way and deserving of an education that meets their individual needs. From what we've seen, teachers who believe in learning styles are also often the ones most willing to put in the extra work of tailoring lessons to match student needs. Clearly, teachers who do this love teaching, love their students, and try their hardest to individualize instruction to make it more effective.

Additionally, it's important to remember that we may not all mean the same thing when we talk about learning styles. We have met teachers who believed that they were teaching to learning styles when they were in fact simply teaching in creative ways, using multiple modalities—and with great success. Teaching to what they believed were learning styles actually led these teachers to provide content in multiple ways, or to differentiate teaching, or to appropriately respond when they noticed that a student needed a different kind of exposure. But these lessons were effective not because they were tailored to learning styles, but because they were multimodal and responsive to student needs.

Positive Alternatives to Teaching to Learning Styles

In this section, we will review alternatives to teaching to learning styles that actually achieve the intended purpose of providing students with better access to content and to more targeted ways of learning. There are two powerhouse concepts just waiting to be embraced by thoughtful teachers dedicated to serving students and meeting their needs. These are *metacognition* and *multimodal teaching* that is informed by the targeted content.

Metacognition

Metacognition refers to the act of thinking about thinking. Its practical application in classrooms is to help students learn about how they learn and to help them be intentional about the process of learning. Students who are aware of their thinking can strategically plan for how best to go about the process of learning. Having students analyze their "learning styles" may feel like we are helping them develop metacognition, but by doing so, we may have the opposite effect. A student may have preferences and strengths in certain areas and be aware of these, but that doesn't mean that the student will benefit from having learning funneled through these modalities. With regard to the teaching, the nature of the content ought to play the determining role in how that content is best presented. We'll address this in more depth when we talk about multimodal teaching. With regard to the learning, we ought to be supporting students in the development of metacognition in a way that helps them be more proactive about making sense of content.

A belief in learning styles can actually prevent students from being strategic about their own learning—the self-limiting perception Dweck (2006) identified and that we have seen from advisees looking for us to sign course withdrawal cards. Metacognition should open doors rather than close them. It ought to serve as a catalyst that directs students toward strategies like self-questioning, self-monitoring, and understanding how best to organize information when studying for a test. Helping students focus on metacognition empowers them to take ownership of their learning and to strategically approach challenging tasks (Hattie, 2009).

Let's look now at a few ways to support metacognition.

Strategic prompts

The key to helping students develop metacognition is to help them focus on the learning process and their role in it, and then connect them to various actions they might take in various circumstances. This might include helping them identify the challenge they are facing, think through solutions they might try, and reflect on the actions they've taken and the various outcomes they've achieved. Teachers can assist students in thinking about their thinking using simple prompts that surround the learning process. The strategic reader prompts in Figure 2.1 are one way to help students engage in metacognition while improving their reading. Teachers can stop and ask students to answer one or more prompts before they begin a reading task.

While some students are self-starters, some need to be guided through the process of seeing themselves as learners, which is the first step in metacognition. To this end, Figure 2.2 presents various prompts for helping students plan for completing a project or assignment.

Figure 2.1—Strategic Reading Prompts

Planning: *Before You Read*

- What is your plan for making sense of this text? (Ideas: take notes, highlight, use sticky notes, turn the headings into questions and try to answer them, or try another approach that has worked for you in the past)
- What text features can help you better understand what you read? (Examples of text features are graphs, pictures, and bold print.)
- What has worked for you that you might want to use again?

Monitoring: *While You Read*

- Are you understanding what you are reading?
- Are you able to picture what you are reading?
- Are you creating questions as you read?
- Are you able to summarize what you just read?
- What will you do if you don't understand something?
- What sense-making strategies are working for you?

Reflecting: *After You Read*

- Did you understand what you read?
- What questions do you have?
- What were your areas of confusion?
- What did you do to better understand the confusing parts?
- What sense-making strategies worked for you?

Figure 2.2—Strategic Planning Prompts for Projects or Assignments

Planning: *Ideas for Getting Started*

- List some ideas for how you will get off to a good start.
- How will you know when you're ready to begin work?
- Pretend that you or your friend completed the project or assignment and did a great job. What did the completed piece look like? What ideas does that give you?

Monitoring: *While You Work*

- What is your projected timeline for how you hope things will go?
- What will you do to keep your progress on track?
- What will you do if you encounter difficulty or setbacks?

Reflecting: *After You Finish*

- How will you determine if your work on this assignment was successful? What are the measures of success you will look at?

Time trackers

Focusing students on metacognition can also bring them an awareness of how long it takes them, at present, to complete projects, which they can then use to guide their work on longer-term assignments and to refine their study habits. Indeed, the ability to manage time effectively may even be more predictive of college grades than SAT scores (Britton & Tesser, 1991). The time tracker in Figure 2.3 is aimed at helping students both anticipate the amount of time a project or assignment will take and monitor how much time it actually does take. The information gathered is data to consider—further fuel for metacognition. Developing metacognitive skills is a long-term investment. It prepares students to understand how to monitor their own learning as a continuous effort, as opposed to applying a one-and-done label related to a learning style. With regard to how students view themselves as learners, metacognition moves them toward an active growth mindset rather than toward a passive fixed mindset (Dweck, 2006).

Figure 2.3—Time Management Tracker

Use this simple tool to help yourself manage the time you spend on an assignment.

Record the time you begin the assignment.

Start time:______________________________

How long do you think this assignment should take? Record the expected time you should end.

Idea: Set a timer to help yourself stay focused.

Planning to end at:________________________

Record the actual time it took you to complete this assignment.

Actual end time:_________________________

How did it go? Why?

Once you get the hang of this, use this same technique to keep track of your start and end times. Jot these down on the margins of your assignments or on sticky notes.

Note-taking guides

Research tells us that students' performance improves when they know how to effectively take notes (Evans & Shively, 2019; Lee et al., 2008), and that students who summarize what they hear in a lecture are much more effective at learning content than those who try to copy notes verbatim (Lahtinen et al., 1997). But students won't necessarily know this is the case unless we tell them, and they aren't likely to practice summarizing their notes unless we guide them to do so. Figure 2.4 is a simple template that students can copy into their notebooks to help them more effectively take notes by thinking about and summarizing notes they take instead of just trying to capture what they read or hear word for word.

Figure 2.4—Note-Taking Template

NOTES	THOUGHTS ON NOTES
• *Record your notes in this column.* • *Unless it's a specific quote that you need, use your own words to capture the main thoughts being shared.*	• *Jot down a summary, questions, or thoughts about the notes you've taken.* • *Do you understand your notes?* • *Can you picture what's in your notes?*

Reflection guides

Teachers can guide students to reflect on their own learning by asking them to jot down their thoughts after reading or completing an assignment. One teacher we know asked his students to record reflections on the back of an assignment before they submitted it. It was a powerful add-on that only took a few minutes and allowed students to see themselves as active creators of their own learning.

The survey in Figure 2.5 provides prompts to help learners engage in metacognitive reflection.

Figure 2.5—Student Survey: Post-Assignment Reflection

1. What challenge(s) did you experience with this assignment?

2. How did you address the challenges(s). What worked for you? What didn't?

3. What are you noticing about yourself as a learner?

Multimodal Teaching That Suits the Content

There is a lot to gain by paying more attention to the commonalities students share rather than the ways in which they are different. "We are all visual learners, and we are all auditory learners, not just some of us," write Hattie and Yates (2014). "Laboratory studies reveal that we all learn well when the inputs we experience are multimodal or conveyed through different media . . . [or] when words and images are combined" (p. 115). Teaching all students multimodally rather than using different forms of instruction with different students is a positive and powerful alternative to learning style theory.

What does this look like? Well, first, we need to remember that the work of designing any learning task begins not with the specifics of a task (including its modalities) but with the desired learning outcomes as they specifically connect to the content. Ultimately, what do we want our students to know, to understand, to be able to do at the completion of the lesson? Always start with your content goal, visualize it, and then select the best delivery method or methods. For example, as you plan, think about the following questions:

Visual Components

- Would your presentations be better with visuals of the content?
- Would it help if all students drew images that represent the concrete or abstract content?

Auditory Components

- Would it help if you prepared a directed teaching presentation on this content?
- Would it help for all students to articulate their understandings of the content?

Kinesthetic and Sensorimotor Components

- Would it help if you employed movement or the use of muscle memory that is tied to the meaning of the content?
- Would it help for all students to create actions or gestures that are tied to the meaning of the content?

Regarding kinesthetic learning, note that theorists define the kinesthetic modality differently (see Fleming & Mills, 1992; Willingham, 2015). Willingham (2005) defines it as requiring muscle memory to assist in learning. For example, assuming we could dance, we could verbally describe for you the steps to certain dance moves ("a three-quarter turn of your hip toward the front left big toe"), and we could even show you pictures of those steps, but nothing would work better than modeling moves for you as you practiced them yourself.

Combining modalities is helpful for all students, regardless of perceived learning styles. Here's an example. When teaching number sense with 1st graders, Pérsida wanted her students to be able to picture numbers not only as numerically written characters but also within the logical order of numerical values that follows a predictable repeated pattern. To support that goal, she used, among other tools, unifix cubes, oral number stories (word problems), a large chart paper–sized 100s chart, and laminated individual student copies of that same chart.

Pérsida didn't just want students to hear about 10s units using an auditory modality; she wanted them to hear, see, and construct representations that helped them understand that, after 10 numbers in a row, the number line begins again in a consistent pattern. These instructional goals drove her choice of modalities, not any assumptions about individual learning differences. The 100s chart allowed all students to see how numbers worked in a logical order and that that there existed both vertical and horizontal patterns: for example, students colored in their laminated sheets to show that multiples of five were consistent down the center and end rows. Pérsida also used sticky notes to cover numbers on the large 100s chart and asked students to determine which numbers were missing. She then asked them to use their fingers to "write" the numbers on the carpet, share it with a neighbor, and then, at her signal, shout it out at the top of their lungs. Later, after some modeling, at their seats, the students assembled cubes in groups of 10s as Pérsida called out random numbers. For example, if she called out 33, the students lined up three rows of 10s, one beneath the other, and assembled the three single blocks in the row below. Pérsida wanted them to see and construct visual representations of the abstract numerals so they could develop basic number sense.

This multimodal type of lesson is especially helpful for English learners because it helps them learn both language and content at the same time while including frequent checks for understanding. Using both auditory and visual modalities allowed *all* of Pérsida's students to hear oral word problems, understand them, and grasp how the numbers worked in logical and orderly patterns. Kinesthetic activities that make use of muscle memory (to pick one example common among learning style proponents) just don't lend themselves to number sense as easily as a simple 100s chart, number stories, and unifix cubes do. And if Pérsida had omitted the visual piece of her lesson on the assumption that it didn't match specific students' learning styles, her lessons would have been dramatically less effective. Even students who have better auditory than visual memories needed to *see* how the numbers were ordered.

It is important to note that content-related memories are not usually stored as words, pictures, or movements, but as meaning. For instance, Willingham (2005) describes how learners will inaccurately recognize specific sentences from a story that align with a remembered meaning, even if the sentences never actually appeared in the story. Thus, understanding meaning, not just pictures or just words, ought to be our primary goal when helping students learn content. And as Hattie and Yates (2014) write, "Claims made such that 'some students learn from words, but others learn from images' are incorrect, as all students learn most effectively through linking images with words" (p. 115). Likewise, Boser (2019) notes that "[p]sychological research has established that integrating text and visuals together is often a more effective way of delivering information than providing text and visuals separately" (p. 10).

Gestures and role-play may also enhance learning in certain contexts. For example, Andrä and colleagues (2020) found that when children performed gestures and pictures to learn language, their performance improved. "There is mounting evidence that sensorimotor enrichment also increases learning efficiency and memory performance," they write. "We use the term sensorimotor enrichment to indicate the presence of movements such as gestures during learning that are semantically congruent with information presented in another sensory modality" (p. 816). *Semantically congruent* refers to a movement that is tied to the meaning of the word in a way that makes sense. For example, movements linked to the word *expansive* would emphasize its large size. Students using multisensory approaches in this study were still able to recall meanings of words a full six months after they had been taught.

Conclusion

Many teachers believe that helping students understand their learning styles is much the same as helping them develop metacognitive skills. But learning styles and metacognition are quite different, and students who believe they can only learn in a certain way might be dissuaded from learning other helpful strategies for understanding content. While catering to student learning preferences in order to support student success is a noble goal, research fails to support the efficacy of this approach to achieve that end. Because all students are visual *and* auditory learners, it's better, the research tells us, to use multiple modes of delivery based on what works best for the content being taught (Hattie & Yates, 2014; Pashler et al., 2007; Willingham, 2018).

3

Homework as the Default

There's no crying in baseball!
A League of Their Own, 1992

We'll admit it: we used to be sold on the idea of homework. It sounded so good! Who wouldn't love extra time for students to practice both the skills they are learning in class and how to act like responsible adults? Like many teachers, we believed the assumptions commonly shared about homework—that it extends learning (by extending the school day), improves achievement, builds time-management capacity, improves study skills, and supports children on their way to becoming responsible adults.

We thought homework was great . . . until we had children of our own. Then the tears came, along with the feelings of incompetence, the negativity, more tears, thinly veiled references to running away, and some quietly mumbled cusswords. And that was just from us! When we say, "There's no crying in baseball," we're looking at you, moms and dads, as well as at your kids and at ours.

Unlike other practices addressed in this book, which a clear consensus of experts have spoken out against, the topic of homework is controversial and complex. We have come to believe that if homework is assigned, it should be assigned not automatically but *judiciously,* with a clear understanding of the potential consequences that homework may have, especially for our most vulnerable student populations. In this chapter, we dig into the controversy and present our case for a more thoughtful approach toward assigning homework.

What's Problematic About Homework as the Default?

Warnings about how homework can negatively affect students and families have been with us for more than a hundred years. "A century or so ago," writes Pinsker (2019), "progressive reformers argued that [homework] made kids unduly stressed, which later led, in some cases, to district-level bans on it for all grades under seventh" (para. 1). As far back as the early 1900s, the risks associated with homework were seen by many as far outweighing any benefits. Back then, Vatterott (2018) writes, "homework was blamed for nervous conditions in children, eyestrain, stress, lack of sleep, and other conditions" (p. 4). As Gill and Schlossman (2004) note, complaints and arguments about homework are still very much with us and "tend—as much today as in the past—toward extreme, angry, often contradictory views" (p. 174).

Robinson and Aronica (2018) aptly captured the literature on homework when they titled an article "How Much Homework Is Enough? Depends on Who You Ask." Most experts agree that studies have yet to show any conclusive benefits to assigning homework in the elementary grades (Bennett & Kalish, 2006; Hattie, 2009; Kohn, 2006b; Vatterott, 2018). Those who conclude that homework is worthwhile acknowledge that it also has the potential to turn students off the process of learning (Cooper, 1989; Cooper et al., 2006; Marzano & Pickering, 2007). Other researchers point to evidence that homework may have negative effects on students' overall well-being (Galloway et al., 2013; Pressman et al., 2015; Terada, 2018). For an encapsulation of the potential dangers associated with homework for students who struggle most with it, we'll quote John Hattie (2009): "Homework reinforces that [students] cannot learn by themselves, and that they cannot do the schoolwork. For these students, homework can undermine motivation, internalize incorrect routines and strategies, and reinforce less effective study habits, especially for elementary students" (p. 235).

Alfie Kohn (2015) takes a strong stand against homework. "No research has ever found a benefit to assigning homework (of any kind or in any amount) in elementary school," he writes. "If we're making 12-year-olds, much less 5-year-olds, do homework, it's either because we're misinformed about what the evidence says, or because we think kids ought to have to do homework despite what the evidence says" (p. 106). After analyzing established research studies, Kohn found no evidence of any academic benefits associated with homework in either the elementary or middle grades and only weak support for its use in the secondary grades. In his work, Kohn takes aim at several researchers who endorse the use of homework, including Marzano and Pickering (2007), who counter that "the research on homework supports its use even at the elementary level, but it does not support its improper use. Homework must be structured in a way that students can accomplish it with relatively high success rates, so that they will complete all or large portions of the homework" (p. 513).

John Hattie (2009) asserts that, while homework has been found to benefit high school students, its effect on the academic achievement of elementary students is nil. While he does not support abolishing homework in the elementary grades, he does support schools working with parents to ensure that all elementary homework is meaningful (Professional Learning Supports, 2014).

With the broad lines of the controversy thus drawn, let's take a closer look and examine the implications for policy and the effects of homework on students and families.

The Cooper Studies and Their Influence

One of the leading names in homework research is Harris Cooper, who conducted two influential meta-analyses (Cooper, 1989; Cooper et al., 2006). Many of the homework policies in effect today can be traced back to Cooper's work, including the popular "10-minute rule": 10 minutes of homework in 1st grade, with an additional 10 minutes for each subsequent grade level, culminating in two hours of homework in 12th grade. While the National PTA has historically supported this rule, it should be noted that the organization put out a resolution endorsing quality over quantity of homework in 2016.

Cooper's 1989 meta-analysis reviewed nearly 120 empirical studies of homework, all of which, he acknowledges, had identifiable design flaws. His conclusion was that "homework has a positive effect on achievement, but the effect varies dramatically with grade level. For high school students, homework has substantial benefits. Junior high school students also benefit from homework, but only about half as much. For elementary school students, the effect of homework on achievement is negligible" (p. 88). Despite these findings, Cooper recommends "that elementary school students be given homework, even though it should not be expected to improve test scores. Instead, homework for young children should help them develop good study habits, foster positive attitudes toward school, and communicate to students the idea that learning takes place at home as well as at school" (p. 90). But Alfie Kohn (2006b) emphasizes that there is no evidence that homework helps teach children self-discipline or responsibility, and Hattie (2009) finds no evidence that it helps them develop time-management skills. In 2006, Cooper and colleagues released a meta-analysis of studies on homework published between 1987 and 2003 that draws similar conclusions.

Vatterott (2018) and Kohn (2006a) both warn that official policies and long-held beliefs about homework may be overly reliant on Cooper's two meta-analyses. In an article provocatively titled "Abusing Research," Kohn pulls no punches, going so far as to accuse Cooper of misrepresenting research findings: "a careful reading of Cooper's own studies—as opposed to his research reviews—reveals further examples of his determination to massage the numbers until they yield something—anything—on which to construct a defense of homework for younger children" (2006a, p. 19).

In that same article, Kohn discusses data from National Assessment of Educational Progress (NAEP) and Trends in International Mathematics and Science Study (TIMSS) tests that show an ambiguous relationship between the amount of homework a student is assigned and higher test scores. For 4th graders who did 45 minutes of math homework, NAEP scores declined; for 8th graders, scores improved with 15 to 45 minutes of homework but declined with over an hour's worth. For 12th graders, scores were similar for those who did 15 minutes of homework and those who did more than an hour.

How Homework Affects Families

One of the assumptions regarding homework is that it will support parental involvement and play a positive role in informing parents about the content their children are learning. But there is research that throws these assumptions into question. Pressman and colleagues (2015) found that family stress and tension increase as caregivers' comfort levels with assisting with homework decrease. "Homes with higher rates of stress and tension are more likely to have adults and children arguing over homework," they write, "as well as children who dislike their homework" (p. 306). The researchers also found that Spanish-speaking homes experienced more homework-related stress than English-speaking ones. "The disproportionate homework load for K–3 found in our study calls into question whether primary school children are being exposed to a positive learning experience or to a scenario that may promote negative attitudes toward learning" (p. 308).

In their book *The Case Against Homework* (2006), Bennett and Kalish provide parents with practical tips for advocating against homework on behalf of their children. The fact that there is a market for such a book is in itself telling. A *Washington Post Book World* endorsement on the back cover describes the book as "a battlefield manual for parents." Are educators really *battling* against parents? Do parents see us as their enemy? Do they see us as their children's enemy?

We join with Vatterott (2018) in urging all educators to "embrace parents as equal partners in their child's education." However, we also agree with Vatterott when she goes on to say that "the role of parents in homework must be voluntary, respectful, and individualized, and the value of family life must be honored" (p. 63).

"It doesn't make sense to me that the school can send something home that makes your kid miserable, that interferes with your family time, and that interferes with your child's developing into a whole, complex person," notes Sara Bennett, a criminal defense appeals attorney who writes on the topic of homework, in an interview with Kate McReynolds (2007).

"And to top it off, they can't even show that homework has any value. They can make up a reason—responsibility, self-discipline, motivation—but that doesn't mean that it has any basis in fact" (p. 14).

As noted, a study by Pressman and colleagues (2015) reported that families with less educational attainment and families in high-poverty neighborhoods feel less able to support their children with homework. The finding leads the authors to ask an important question:

> Ought a parent to be involved in a child's homework at the instructional level? The conundrum relates to educational inequities among public school students who come from families with one parent, whose parent may be unavailable at homework time, and/or may not have the education, temperament, or language proficiency to assist the child vs. students who come from families with two parents, one or both of whom are available, and may have educational training and/or temperament to provide their children with instruction. It may be argued that the expectation that parents provide instructive guidance to a child with his homework, would be, through no fault of the child, a benefit to some children and a detriment to others. (p. 309)

Whether or not children complete their homework is largely due to whether or not parents have the time, ability, or knowledge to force the issue (e.g., "No video games until you finish your homework!"). Unfortunately, we "continue to disproportionately fail students from lower-income households for not doing homework, in essence punishing them for lack of an adequate environment in which to do homework" (Vatterott, 2018, p. 2). Instead of thinking, "That child always does his homework," we ought to think, "That child has parents who make sure he always does his homework." Do we really want to be grading or penalizing students for what their parents do or don't do?

How Homework Affects Student Well-Being

Galloway and colleagues (2013) found that too much homework carries risks to overall well-being. Their study concluded that high school students in privileged high-performing classrooms who were given an average of three hours of nightly homework may have gained a competitive academic edge, but only at the cost of less sleep, more academic stress, poorer health, and a perceived lack of school–life balance. "Given the pressure students in such advantaged, high-achieving communities feel to achieve academically," the researchers wrote, "the open-ended data suggest that many students feel forced or obligated to choose homework over developing other talents or skills" (p. 506). Galloway and colleagues challenge the assumption that homework is "inherently good." Regardless of its intended benefits, they write, homework means "young people are spending more time alone, which means less time for family and fewer opportunities to engage in their community" (p. 506). The study also notes that grading students on homework completion rewards mere compliance over genuine understanding.

A growing body of evidence points to an increase in depression and mental health–related issues among young people (Duffy et al., 2019; Keyes et al., 2019; Mojtabai et al., 2016). Comparing data from 2003–2006 with data from 2014–2017, Livingston (2019) found that teens are spending less time socializing and doing paid work and more time sleeping and doing homework. According to Livingston, teens spend about an hour per day on homework—15 minutes more than they did a decade ago and 30 minutes more than they did during the 1990s. In Livingston's analysis, "the biggest chunk of teens' daily leisure time is spent on screens: 3 hours and 4 minutes on average. This figure, which can include time spent gaming, surfing the web, watching videos and watching TV, has held over the past decade" (2019, para. 4).

Positive Alternatives to Homework as a Default

While we are not ready to come down on the side of banning all homework, we do find ourselves firmly against assigning homework automatically without consideration of its purpose, efficacy, or potential ill effects on students and their families. Homework for students in the elementary grades poses particular problems, and teachers ought to be especially judicious about assigning it for young students.

Here are some positive alternatives we suggest.

Assign Homework with Intention

The first and perhaps best alternative to automatic homework is occasional and deliberate homework. This begins with reflecting on your current habits and expectations about homework. What do you ask students to do at home? What kind of family support or instructional guidance do you expect students to access at home? What consequences might your requirements and expectations have on your students and their home environments?

We've already mentioned some ways in which homework is especially challenging for students from non-English-speaking or low-socioeconomic backgrounds, but it's an issue worth repeating. "For too many students, homework reinforces that they cannot learn by themselves, and that they cannot do the schoolwork," writes Hattie (2009). "For these students, homework can undermine motivation, internalize incorrect routines and strategies, and reinforce less effective study habits, especially for elementary students" (p. 235). When it comes to your most vulnerable students, homework can actually lower their confidence in themselves as learners, lessen their motivation, and reinforce strategies that you will then have to spend time un-teaching.

Before assigning homework, ask yourself the following questions:

- Is this homework assignment necessary? Why?
- Can all students complete this homework within a reasonable amount of time? If not, how will you differentiate the task so that students spend their time on it productively?
- What will happen if a student cannot complete this assignment? How will you help that student?
- Does the assignment undermine motivation and interest in this topic?
- Would this assignment be more quickly and accurately completed in school?

Keep in mind that the kind of homework assignments that have the most positive effect on learning involve practice, rehearsal, and application of basic skills in fresh contexts rather than deeper or high-level conceptual thinking, which benefits from the guiding presence of a teacher. As Hattie (2009) writes, "The [benefits of homework] were highest in mathematics, and lowest in science and social studies. The effects were higher when the material was not complex or if it was novel" (p. 235). For older students, activities that require deeper learning are best reserved for classroom teaching opportunities, where students can interact with teachers and with one another.

Rethink Assumptions About Parental Involvement

During a recent presentation, a teacher asked us for advice about what to do when a child isn't getting academic support at home. "How do you deal with situations where parents are not making sure the kid's homework is completed or can't help their child with it?" she asked. This question laid bare three assumptions every teacher ought to reassess.

1. **"Helping with homework is the best way parents can support students."** The best kind of family support for a child is, of course, a safe and loving home. Coming home from school should feel like a warm hug, with caregivers asking students about their day and opportunities to go outside and play. After-school reading should also be a time of relaxation, without the phony technicalities of reading logs and book reports getting in the way.
2. **"Parents should make sure that students complete their homework."** While this may sound like a no-brainer to some, we know from personal experience how much tension being a homework monitor can cause in a household. Many days, we had to spend our time badgering, redirecting, and reprimanding our kids until they finished their homework, and this sucked a lot of joy out of our fleeting family time. Making sure that homework is completed is more taxing than it sounds.
3. **"Parents should take on an instructional role at home."** Even Harris Cooper (1989) warned against this assumption. We should never depend on parents to take on the role of teachers. Not only does this place vulnerable students at risk, it also weakens the self-efficacy of parents, who should be deciding for themselves what to do during family time and whose main role should be raising healthy and well-loved kids.

We want parents to talk with their children and, if possible, to read with them. But we don't expect parents to instruct them or monitor their homework. This is a heavy burden to place on them, especially if they work late hours or don't have a basic command of English. Instead, we want parents to spend time with their children and to ask their children quality questions about school.

By using our in-class time strategically and embedding formative assessments throughout our lessons, we can render homework assignments unnecessary. Alfie Kohn (2006b) advises that instead of assigning homework as a default, we only do so when there is a compelling reason for it: "as a matter of classroom practice, students should be asked to take schoolwork home only when there's a reasonable likelihood that a particular assignment will be beneficial to most of them" (p. 166).

Support Healthy After-School Habits

Teachers should examine the limitations we place on students who are actively involved in extracurricular activities, work part-time jobs (developing valuable people skills), or spend their time in social, religious, or community activities. If students are too busy engaging with their communities to do their homework, might that be a *good* thing? A cause for applause rather than a reason to be penalized? Based on what you know about your students, consider creating some room to support the development of healthy habits unrelated to the classroom.

Communicate Your Expectations

If you decide to modify your homework policies (or eliminate homework altogether), let parents know as soon as you can. Give parents your rationale. Be frank with them. Feel free to directly quote the material in this chapter if you'd like. If you'll still be periodically sending things home (e.g., rote memorization or simple practice assignments), let parents know that, too. Share with them any suggested time limits for homework. And if, instead of dealing with homework, you want parents to support their children by discussing content or reading materials with them, then say so.

Encourage At-Home Reading

Many studies link the amount of time spent reading with increases in vocabulary acquisition (Cunningham & Stanovich, 2001; Elley, 1989, 1991,

2000; Krashen, 2004; Nagy et al., 1985). Because vocabulary development is critical for students' success in all aspects of school, not just in English classes, *reading is probably the most important thing parents can do to help their children succeed academically.* It's important that we help parents understand this when we meet with them at back-to-school nights or parent events.

Family lending libraries

Camille Hopkins, a principal in Lancaster, Pennsylvania, established a family lending library in the building where parents could sign out books for their children. The library was conveniently located near the front office so that parents would not need to gain access to the rest of the building when taking out books. During the pandemic, the physical library expanded to contain virtual access to e-books and audiobooks. The audiobooks played an especially important role in the lives of students whose parents did not feel comfortable reading longer chapter-books to their children. Every year, Hopkins introduces the importance of family reading and its impact on school achievement to students and their families. She re-introduces the lending library every year during back-to-school nights and brings it up at monthly parent–teacher organization meetings. If we want to encourage family reading, we will also want to make it as easy as possible for all families to have access to books.

Motivation and social interactions around books

It's important to focus on motivating students to read, rather than mandating that they read, and enlisting parents as enforcers in this effort. Yes, this is a reference to the widespread use of "reading logs." With typical reading logs, students are directed to read for a certain amount of time at home each night, and parents are asked to "sign off" in a date-marked notebook to confirm that the reading was completed. One parent we spoke to described how her son would set a kitchen timer for the required 20 minutes. He would read until the exact moment the timer went off, then jump up to get his mother's initials as the timer buzzed loudly in the background. He took no time to reflect on what he had read or even to finish the sentence he was reading when the timer went off. What a way to kill any sense of joy around reading! Another mom described to us how her child would incessantly ask, "Is my time up?" until she threatened to add five minutes for every time he asked. How's that for building motivation to read? What's more, we know a few teachers who have complained that their students' weekly reading logs suspiciously seem to have been initialed with the same writing instrument at the same time (often the night before the due date), indicating that the parents weren't really monitoring their children's reading at all.

Mandatory reading logs may be meant to encourage reading, but they do not. Pak and Weseley (2012) compared reading motivation among 2nd and 3rd graders who were assigned to groups using either mandatory or volunteer reading logs. As you might expect, students in the former group showed less motivation to read than their peers in the latter group.

What does increase reading motivation? According to Linda Gambrell (2011), the answer is student choice and social interactions around text. This conclusion is supported by 5th grade teacher and author Allie Thrower (2019), who describes how she structured learning interactions to increase both how much time students spent reading and how motivated they were to read. She ditched the reading logs in favor of "accountability partners": after reading at home, students would spend 10 minutes the next day in class discussing the book with a classmate. Thrower's anecdotal evidence supports the idea that when students interact socially around text, they get excited about reading.

Encourage Parent–Student Talk

One common belief about homework is that it increases parental involvement in their children's education. But the research presents conflicting evidence on whether or not this is true. As noted, we know that homework can actually take a toll on families across socioeconomic levels. While Pressman and colleagues (2015) talk about the impact on families of lower socioeconomic means, Bennett and Kalish's (2006) audience seem to have quite a bit of agency. But one simple thing we can do to support healthy home environments is to provide tips for increasing the amount of time parents and children simply talk with one another. Consider sharing a set of simple prompts, in both English and relevant home languages, that parents can use to jump-start daily dialogues with kids after school. These examples are modified from Soukup (2020):

- What was your high point today?
- What was your low point today?
- What is something interesting that you learned in school today?

These prompts, which can be easily transferred to a handy bookmark and reviewed with children, would probably do more to inform parents of what is happening in school than expecting them to assist with or take note of their children's homework.

Do "the Important Stuff" in School (Yes, This Includes Reading)

The presence of teachers and peers during academic experiences can substantially increase student learning (Hattie, 2009). "[W]hen homework and in-class study were compared in elementary schools," writes Cooper (1989), "in-class study actually proved superior" (p. 88). So if you really want students to learn something, have them learn it in school, where you are around to assist, clarify, and prompt as needed.

Even homework assignments that are meant to simply provide practice may benefit from your presence. And having students complete assignments at school is a way for teachers to ensure that students get the formative feedback necessary to meet their academic needs. Remember that, in general, the students who need the most help are the ones who face the most difficulty completing homework, through no fault of their own. Furthermore, because we are not present when homework is being completed, we risk unfairly penalizing students, especially young students, when homework is graded instead of used as an opportunity to practice simple skills.

We stand by the belief that reading is important enough to do in school, and there are data that support this belief. However, this principle was thrown into question during the past few decades, leading many schools to ban sustained silent reading (SSR) during the height of No Child Left Behind (NCLB). A 2000 review of 14 experimental studies by the National Reading Panel (NRP) concluded that in-class time set aside for silent reading did not raise reading skills and fluency, but Garan and DeVoogd (2008) take issue with the NRP's conclusion, arguing that the 14 studies upon which the National Reading Panel's recommendations were made ignored hundreds of other studies supporting SSR. “In other words,” they write, “there were hundreds of studies to support SSR, but because they did not meet the panel’s narrow selection criteria, the NRP excluded them” (p. 338).

As you can imagine, the NRP’s findings dealt a damaging blow to the practices of sustained silent reading times in many classrooms, and likely an even more damaging blow to schools in low-income neighborhoods whose daily regimen of standardized test–based reading practices left no time for getting lost in a good book.

Garan and DeVoogd are far from alone in their criticisms of the NRP’s findings. According to a joint statement by the International Reading Association (now the International Literacy Association [ILA]), the Canadian Children’s Book Centre (CCBC), and the National Council of Teachers of English (NCTE), the NRP analysis has “been used to support policy initiatives that lead to a decrease in classroom leisure reading. The goals of fostering a love of reading and developing a lifelong habit of reading for pleasure have been supplanted by the goal of supporting students’ performance on high-stakes literacy tests” (IRA et al., 2014, p. 3). The NRP recommendations were highly disputed by many other literacy experts as well (e.g., Allington, 2011; Cunningham, 2001; Edmondson & Shannon, 2002; Gallagher, 2009; Krashen, 2005; Sanden, 2014; and numerous others).

Stephen Krashen refers to silent reading as “free voluntary reading” (FVR) because it involves student choice, which is known to increase motivation (Gambrell, 2011; Krashen, 2004). As Krashen (2004) explains, “FVR means reading because you want to. For school-aged children, FVR means no book report, no questions at the end of the chapter, and no looking up every vocabulary word” (p. x). This is how adults read books. Is it any wonder that children would prefer this as well? This kind of reading experience is much too important to be left up to chance, so we must allow students time to engage in it at school.

It’s also important to provide opportunities for students to share what they are reading through structured techniques that provide accountability without feeling forced. Simply giving students a specific prompt that they can use to discuss what they’ve read can help in this way and can even generate interest among students in the books their classmates are reading. Here are a few examples of prompts you can use after silent reading time in your own classroom:

Discussion Prompts for Narrative Texts

- What did you read about today? Describe what the book is about, but don't give away the ending.
- Describe your favorite or least favorite character. What events in the story led you to like or dislike this character?
- Think of people in your life. Whom might the characters represent in your life? Whom are they most like? Whom are you most like? Explain why, using specific examples.
- How are everyday issues reflected in this book?
- Suppose you were to adapt this text into a movie. Describe the kind of music or soundtrack you would use for the various parts. Explain why.
- How did the author use language to create more vivid images in your mind? Share an example.

Discussion Prompts for Informational Texts

- What did you read about today? Describe the text in detail. If you have a favorite excerpt, read it to your classmate.
- What issues does the text raise?
- What questions does the text leave unanswered?
- What kind of people would like or dislike, or agree or disagree with the text? Explain your thinking.
- Suppose you were to create a documentary about this text. Describe the kind of music or soundtrack you would use for the various parts. Explain why.
- How did the author use language to create more vivid images in your mind? Share an example.

Keep these discussions short; pick just one prompt, ask students to share in pairs or small groups, then ask for volunteers who'd like to share out with the whole class. You may also want to consider weekly reading circles, where you ask students to join you in small groups to share their texts. After posing a prompt, make sure to let students do most of the talking.

Ask Students for Input

"Teachers who consult with their students on a regular basis would shake their heads vigorously were you to suggest that kids will always say no to homework—or to anything else that requires effort," writes Alfie Kohn (2007). "It's just not true, they'll tell you. When students are treated with respect, when the assignments are worth doing, most kids relish a challenge" (para. 20). We saw this firsthand in our own classrooms. When children were excited about a topic or project, they'd volunteer to work on it at home.

If you're not sure about what kind of homework assignments motivate your students, ask them. Use the survey in Figure 3.1 to ask students for their thoughts on homework assignments that have worked for them in the past. If you decide that the surveys should be anonymous, explain that to students. Otherwise, be sure to explain that they won't be penalized for anything they say and that you really want their honest opinions.

Figure 3.1—Student Survey: Homework

1. How do you feel about homework in general?
2. Have you ever really liked a specific homework assignment or project? What about it did you like?
3. Have you ever really disliked a specific homework assignment or project? What about it did you dislike?
4. If you could give some advice to your teachers about homework, what would you say?

Conclusion

To us, the research seems clear: *homework should not be a daily requirement,* especially not in the elementary grades. It ought to be assigned only when there is a compelling reason to do so, and it ought to be simple and short. Students should know what they need to do and how they need to do it without requiring parental assistance. Pressman and colleagues (2015) point to evidence that the well-being of both parents and children may suffer if homework conflicts with meaningful leisure and family routines. "The case for having parental involvement at the instructional level with a child's homework," they write, "appears to be outweighed by negative sociological, emotional, and educational consequences" (p. 309).

As a teacher, you'll want to gauge how your students feel about homework. Do they find it helpful and motivating, or does it make them feel deflated and incapable of learning? Input from your most vulnerable students can be especially consequential, as homework has the unfortunate potential to exacerbate stressful home environments. Ask yourself: is assigning homework worth the troubles it may cause?

Finally, remember that the best thing for all students is a warm and supportive home environment. Every parent, regardless of home language, educational attainment, special needs, literacy skills, or socioeconomic status, can have a positive impact on their child's schooling, and every parent needs to know that.

4

Formative Assessment Imposters

Anyone? Anyone?

Ferris Bueller's Day Off, 1986

Formative assessment—that is, the process of conducting ongoing checks for understanding within the context of classroom lessons—is a powerfully effective teaching practice. As an example, a formative assessment strategy might take the form of a quick-write, where students stop and respond to a prompt related to a teaching presentation and then share those responses in pairs or small groups, with the teacher carefully listening in to gauge students' learning status. This kind of assessment *for* learning (Stiggins & Chappuis, 2006) is and has long been identified as an essential component of student-responsive K–12 instruction. Unfortunately, the term *formative assessment* is often misunderstood by practicing educators to mean simply pausing every once in a while to ask, "Does everybody understand?"

For more than two decades, we've worked to support teachers as they mentor novice practitioners. Every year, we ask mentors to help their mentees identify five examples of formative assessment, and every year, we need to clarify what we mean by the term. We often hear mentions of paper-and-pencil tests and commercial interim assessments. We get responses like "We assess according to the math department schedule" or "We do formative assessments, but we follow the district's progress monitoring due dates." The literature on formative assessment corroborates our perception that teachers rarely implement it as it is described in the education literature and research (Learning Sciences International, 2019; Popham, 2018). But it's hard to address the need for better formative assessment practices if many educators don't even know what formative assessment is.

For most people, teachers included, what comes first to mind when they hear the word *assessment* is "tests"—specifically, scheduled unit tests and periodic district-mandated appraisals of student progress. But unlike summative assessments, which are designed to produce an evaluative *summary* of what students have mastered in the form of a percentage or letter grade, formative assessment is built into lessons by individual teachers for the purpose of *informing,* and potentially *transforming,* instruction. Formative assessment is not asking, "Does everyone understand?" and waiting for responses. As Popham (2018) explains, it's an ongoing process that involves taking continual measurements of understanding and using the data you get to not only adjust your instructional approach but also provide students with feedback they can use to adjust their learning approach—not at the end of the lesson or the unit, and not when the scores come back from the district in two weeks or six weeks, but right now.

Teachers who excel at what they do constantly monitor learning and recalibrate their teaching according to what they see. To them, formative assessment is not a singular event but an ongoing methodology. It's simply what it means to teach well. These teachers don't wait for exam results to tell them who needs help mastering content, because they continuously work at staying aware of who does and doesn't understand. They gauge the extent of students' understanding, and they take steps to provide support, redirection, and reteaching when it is needed. As Wiliam (2007) notes, "If students have left the classroom before the teachers have made adjustments to their teaching on the basis of what they have learned about the students' achievement, then they are already playing catch-up" (p. 191).

What's Problematic About Formative Assessment Imposters?

It's right there in the header. The most problematic thing about "formative assessment imposters" is that they aren't really formative assessment at all and can't do what formative assessment does. Using them may make teachers feel good, but they're not going to produce the powerful results that real formative assessment can produce.

Before we meet the common imposters, let's back up. What *can* formative assessment do? The short answer is "accelerate student growth." The slightly longer answer is "make you a better teacher, and make your students better learners." In one meta-analysis, Black and Wiliam (1998) examined 250 studies and concluded that formative assessment is at the heart of effective teaching:

> All these studies show that innovations that include strengthening the practice of formative assessment produce significant and often substantial learning gains. These studies range over age groups from 5-year-olds to university undergraduates, across several school subjects, and over several countries. . . . Teachers need to know about their pupils' progress and difficulties with learning so that they can adapt their own work to meet pupils' needs—needs that are often unpredictable and that vary from one pupil to another. (p. 140)

Assessment expert James Popham agrees. He refers to formative assessment as a "surefire" approach, pointing to evidence that it may even double the speed of learning. "Recent reviews of related research covering more than 4,000 investigations confirm that formative assessment works—big time" (Popham, 2018, p. 132). Meanwhile, a meta-analysis by John Hattie (2009) found that "feedback was among the most powerful influences on achievement. Most programs and methods that worked best were based on heavy dollops of feedback" (p. 173)—such as the kind teachers receive from formative assessment. "When teachers seek, or at least are open to, feedback from students as to what students know, what they understand, where they make errors, when they have misconceptions, when they are not engaged—then teaching and learning can be synchronized and powerful," Hattie notes. "Feedback to teachers helps make learning visible" (p. 173). A 2019 follow-up to Hattie's meta-analysis found that these conclusions remained sound (Wisniewski et al., 2020).

Wiliam (2007) argues that "the most important difference between the most and the least effective classrooms is the teacher, but the most important variable appears to be what they do, rather than what they know" (p. 186). He describes how the use of formative assessment has been shown to add an extra six to nine months of learning per year, far outweighing the benefits gained from reducing class sizes or increasing teacher content knowledge. Just imagine what six to nine extra months of learning per year could do for your students!

We have yet to meet a teacher or principal who did not want to find effective ways of accelerating student learning, especially the learning of students who are struggling or achieving below grade level. The COVID-19 pandemic has only heightened the importance of this work. Formative assessment is an effective way to achieve these ends and serve all students, especially those who need us most. Unfortunately, the same cannot be said for faux formative assessment.

Imposter #1: Commercial Interim Tests

As the power of formative assessment to support learning was gaining greater attention among educators, commercial publishers began marketing various periodic assessment products as being "formative assessments." Broadly aware that formative assessment was a good thing, but not well versed in how it actually works, these educators came to believe that they were implementing formative assessment in their schools and classrooms when they administered interim tests. While these kinds of formal assessments can be useful in tracking students' progress as they develop key skills over time, Wiliam (2007) notes that "in terms of improving—as opposed to monitoring—student learning, they are almost irrelevant" (p. 191).

By the time an interim assessment is administered, a teacher who has been using formative assessment all along, checking understanding multiple times a day and making continual instructional adjustments, will already know what students need and be providing it. Administering interim assessments according to a schedule fosters a tendency to relegate the task to outsiders, specialists, or paraprofessionals—and this tends to be especially true for students who would benefit the most from authentic formative assessment, like English learners and those receiving special education services. "While formative assessment can help all pupils," write Black and Wiliam (1998), "it yields particularly good results with low achievers by concentrating on specific problems with their work and giving them a clear understanding of what is wrong and how to put it right" (pp. 142–143).

Imposter #2: "Does Everybody Understand?"

We recently sat in on an advanced-level math lesson and were highly impressed by all the content-specific vocabulary flying over our heads. "The *derivative* of the *velocity* gives blah, blah, blah, *acceleration*. . . ." We sat there feeling more and more inadequate with each tick of the clock. "The *integral* blah, blah, *acceleration* blah, blah, blah *velocity*. . . ." This lesson was presented at hyperspeed and included only perfunctory attempts to clear up any misunderstandings in the form of the occasional "Does everybody understand?" After the lesson, we asked a student whether or not she was following along. "Not at all," she said. The teacher, who thought "Does everybody understand?" sufficed to check for understanding, wouldn't know how utterly lost this student was until it came time to score her unit test.

Unfortunately, teachers all over the country think sprinkling their lessons with "Does everybody understand?" is somehow meaningful or effective, even though the question is often met with blank stares and silence. It might even be met with a couple of unrepresentative students' nods. With so little and such undifferentiated student feedback coming in, there's not much to support informed instructional adjustment or feedback to students. "Any questions? Anyone?" is the similarly unhelpful cousin of "Does everybody understand?" It, too, is best avoided.

Imposter #3: The Traditional Q&A

Similar to the periodic question "Does everybody understand?" the traditional Q&A provides teachers with the feeling that they are checking in with students. The misnomer "a class discussion," which is often scribbled into lesson plans, fails to recognize that only a few students are talking. The teacher is busy, animatedly conversing with the handful of participating students, while the majority of the class tries to fly unnoticed beneath the radar.

Picture a typical Q&A session where a teacher stands at the front of the room, asks a question, and calls on volunteers to answer. Now consider the following two Q&A scenarios.

Scenario #1

Teacher: According to your readings, who can tell me why breathing high levels of radon is harmful?

Volunteer A: It's harmful because of the EPA.

Teacher: Not quite. I mean, the EPA stands for the Environmental Protection Agency, and they say it's harmful, but what does radon do?

Volunteer B: It is in the homes?

Teacher: Well, yes, and that is dangerous, right? Why?

Volunteer B: I think it's harmful because it's like a poison.

Teacher: You're on the right track here. How is radon a poison?

[Silence]

Teacher: Well, it's a gas, and it's dangerous because it forms tiny radioactive particles, right? And that's not good. When you breathe them in, these particles can damage your lungs and cause lung cancer. So OK, let's actually get to the topic for today, which is about pollutants and how they form. Let's go back. Who can tell me what radon is?

[Silence]

Teacher: I mean, I just told you, right?

Scenario #2

Teacher: According to your readings, who can tell me why breathing high levels of radon is harmful?

Volunteer A: It's a gas that, like, gets into your house, and it can be dangerous if you breathe a lot of it.

Teacher: Excellent. It's dangerous, and can cause cancer, right? We call these air pollutants. Good. Now let's talk about how a buildup of air pollutants can be prevented.

Teachers who practice the traditional Q&A might feel like Scenario #2 was much more successful than Scenario #1. And that would be true, if the point of a Q&A were to soothe the teacher's ego. But if the point is to teach or review content with the entire class in order to gauge understanding, tease out points of confusion, and reveal and redirect misconceptions, both scenarios fall short of their intent.

In the first scenario, the students' inability to accurately answer the question should alert the teacher to the possibility that the class may not have grasped the concepts of radon and indoor air pollutants. However, this scenario paints a more accurate picture of student understanding than does the second example, which makes it appear as though the class *does* understand the content. In both scenarios, the traditional Q&A "Who can tell me?" prompt leads teachers to make a whole lot of assumptions—first among them that the knowledge of the student who is called on is representative of the classroom's knowledge as a whole. If this student gives the right answer, the rest of the class is off the hook; all 24 of them can breathe a sigh of relief that they won't be put on the spot, even though they may have no clue what their teacher is talking about.

Think, too, about the students who do not raise a hand to answer in either of these scenarios. They might be bored, they might be shy, they might be hesitant with English, or they might need more time to process questions before answering. How does the traditional Q&A help these students at all?

If traditional Q&As are a feature in your classroom, use the survey in Figure 4.1 to solicit formative data in the form of feedback from students on what they think works and what doesn't, then adjust your practice accordingly. If you decide that the surveys should be anonymous, explain that to students. If not, be sure to explain that students won't be penalized and that you really want their honest opinions.

Figure 4.1—Student Survey: Classroom Q&A

1. **I feel like I learn a lot when teachers ask a question to the whole class and then call on students.**

5–strongly agree 4–agree 3–no opinion 2–disagree 1–strongly disagree

Comments:

2. **When teachers ask a question to the whole class and then call on students who raise their hand, I listen carefully to the answer.**

5–strongly agree 4–agree 3–no opinion 2–disagree 1–strongly disagree

Comments:

3. **When teachers ask a question to the whole class and then call on students who did NOT raise their hand, I feel like I am really learning.**

5–strongly agree 4–agree 3–no opinion 2–disagree 1–strongly disagree

Comments:

4. **When I don't understand something, and the teacher finishes a lesson by asking, "Does everybody understand?" I will usually raise my hand to say that I do not understand.**

5–strongly agree 4–agree 3–no opinion 2–disagree 1–strongly disagree

Comments:

5. **If you could give some advice about teaching that involves calling on students or asking, "Does everybody understand?" what would you say?**

Comments:

Positive Alternatives to Formative Assessment Imposters

By the end of every lesson, teachers who use authentic formative assessment have a pretty good feel for which students understand the content and who needs more help. Sarah Collins Lench (2019) reminds educators that the root word of *assess* is *assidere*, meaning "to sit beside." When a teacher *sits beside* a student during formative assessment, the pair are engaged in an interactive dialogue.

But how does one "sit beside" each student in a classroom that has dozens of students? The formative assessment strategies we discuss here will allow you to capture snapshots of what each of your students knows and what each of them needs.

Embed Total Participation Techniques

Several times within every lesson, students should have opportunities to take their developing knowledge and use it in a way that uncovers their understandings for you (and, often, for themselves). Our Total Participation Techniques (TPTs) "are teaching techniques that allow for all students to demonstrate, at the same time, active participation and cognitive engagement in the topic being studied" (Himmele & Himmele, 2017, p. 4).

Total Participation Techniques focus on higher-order prompts for maximum engagement and only include calling on volunteers after each student has had an opportunity to respond to the prompt. Once everyone has responded, calling on volunteers is a richer experience that includes more students. But even students who don't volunteer are still able to provide you with evidence of learning. Following are three TPTs that we have found effective for getting the most out of formative assessment.

Chalkboard Splash

This TPT allows you to get responses to higher-order prompts from all students at the same time. You start by conducting a brief presentation, then pose a deep and meaningful prompt and ask students to jot down their thoughts. Once students are done writing, ask them to write a shorter, condensed version of this response—15 words or less—anywhere on the chalkboard or whiteboard, or add it to a digital bulletin board or digital chat box (Himmele & Himmele, 2017).

We have facilitated and observed Chalkboard Splashes in grades 3 through 12 and with students at the graduate and undergraduate levels. Simple ones can be planned in advance or done on the spot. Although Chalkboard Splashes take as little as five minutes, they generate direct insight into the state of students' understanding.

When the prompt is based on a significantly important aspect of the content we are teaching, we ask students to take another step: gather into small groups of two to four and categorize the responses they and their classmates have generated. For example, at the end of a unit on the Renaissance, students might be asked, "Why is the topic of the Renaissance included in most history curricula? What's the big deal with the Renaissance?" Once the Chalkboard Splash is completed, students in small groups can group their peers' responses into categories provided by the teacher or, if there's more time, generated by the students themselves. For the Renaissance example, categories might include things like economic aspects, cultural aspects, the ushering in of a new era, belief systems, new technologies, and influential advances in the arts, science, and new approaches to learning. Finally, students can be asked to individually create one summation sentence that ties all of their categories together. At the end of a Chalkboard Splash, we've even seen students pull out their phones to photograph the responses generated by their peers to save them as a study tool.

Pause, Star, Rank

In this TPT, students are asked to review the notes they've taken during a lesson and draw stars next to concepts that they think are important. They then rank the top three starred items in order of importance, get together in pairs or small groups, and review their top three items. Students can conduct a Chalkboard Splash with their number-one starred item, or if you have time and are confident that you have developed a cohesive classroom community, a quick way of wrapping up this TPT is by calling on each student, sometimes in order of seating, to read their number-one concept out loud. The safety of having reviewed their starred items in pairs or small groups makes these "call-outs" a bit less intimidating than being randomly called on, but it does rely on the establishment of a safe classroom community that fosters risk taking. The call-outs take a little extra time, but they allow for students to review important concepts and hear their peers' top-ranked responses.

Hold-Ups

In this TPT, students literally hold up their responses to prompts. Hold-Ups work in all grades from kindergarten through 12th grade. For example, younger students can hold up preprinted vowel sounds or digraphs (*sh, th, ch*) to match words the teacher says. In Pérsida's 1st grade classroom, she often used Hold-Ups with three options: True, Not True, and Unable to Determine. After revisiting storybook predictions, when one of her 1st graders pointed out that one prompt was both somewhat true and somewhat *not* true, she added a fourth choice: True with Modifications. At the other end of the K–12 continuum, in Melanie Upton's 12th grade class, students used the exact same response cards to evaluate the intricacies of bioethics. In preselected pairs or small groups, they then elaborated on the card they held up, discussed their rationales, and occasionally changed their minds in response to statements by their peers. Response cards help students show, articulate, and refine their thinking about content and can be easily adapted to virtual settings by having students create the cards and hold them up in front of the camera.

Eschew Random Selection

Think about what is happening in the minds of students waiting to be called on when you randomly select students to answer prompts as a way of checking for understanding. The super-confident students are fine with looking silly. Funny Freddy deflects or makes a joke, the class laughs, Freddy gets the proverbial game-show buzzer sound from the teacher, and it's on to the next student. But what about Attention-Averse Alex and Self-Conscious Susie, who are sitting on opposite sides of Funny Freddy and sweating bullets? They're consumed with how "stupid" they think they will look if called on. Or place yourself in the shoes of your English learners, who have to think not only of the answer but also how to articulate it in English. Consider how much stress these students feel, and how it prevents them from focusing on what you're teaching.

So, while it may seem like a simple solution, we propose that you not randomly call on students. Instead, be sure you've heard your students' responses, perhaps as they're sharing in their small groups, and ask them if it's all right for you to call on them. Tell them that you'd love for them to share what they have to say with the rest of the class. And then, honor their wishes.

Help Students Generate Questions

High school math teacher André Sasser (2018, August 27) shared this wisdom on Twitter: "Two years ago, I was saying 'Do you have any questions?' Last year, I switched to 'What questions do you have?' It made a difference. Today, I tried 'Ask me two questions.' They did! And those questions led to more questions. It amazes me that the littlest things have such a big impact!"

There is, in fact, plenty of evidence that helping students generate questions about what they've learned is a powerful learning strategy with long-term benefits for student retention of information (Ebersbach et al., 2020). This makes sense. Have you ever been in a position where you didn't even know enough to ask a question about what you didn't understand? Asking students to generate questions requires them to review what they know, summarize it with an eye toward knowledge gaps, and then compose questions to which they can pursue solutions. It's a simple, no-frills addition to any lesson that can yield remarkable results. When working virtually, students can easily post these in private chat box comments to their teacher.

Circulate

There's no better way to get immediate feedback from students than to circulate among them as they respond to prompts, discuss their learning in groups, or take notes on lessons. It's so simple, yet so important. Many quieter students will never share in a large-group setting, so you will want to seek them out for feedback and encouragement. When working digitally, be sure to pop in during breakout groups or ask students to use the private messaging feature to share their thoughts before they break off into breakout rooms.

Bill is well known for circulating around his college classroom. His students know that he will be walking among them, occasionally remarking on responses and asking them to elaborate. This helps him to know his students better, and allows them to know Bill better, too. He believes it also allows them to feel more comfortable sharing their response in the larger group.

Focus on Feedback over Grades

"Effective feedback must answer three major questions asked by a teacher and/or by a student," write Hattie and Timperley (2007). "*Where am I going?* (What are the goals?), *How am I going?* (What progress is being made toward the goal?), and *Where to next?* (What activities need to be undertaken to make better progress?)" (p. 86). And it is feedback of this sort, not grades, that helps students understand what they know and what they still need to learn. Conversely, with grades, "the first thing [students] look at is the grade, and the second thing they look at is their neighbor's grade," write Leahy and colleagues (2005). "To be effective, feedback needs to cause thinking. Grades don't do that. Scores don't do that. And comments like 'Good job' don't do that either. What does cause thinking is a comment that addresses what the student needs to do to improve, linked to rubrics where appropriate" (p. 22). Effective feedback provides students with descriptions of what was done well, what needs improvement, and what is noticeably developing, with concrete descriptions of reachable next-level goals.

Pursue Professional Development on Formative Assessment

Data suggest that "investing in teacher professional development is 20–30 times more cost-effective than class-size reduction, at least beyond second grade" (Wiliam, 2007, p. 189). Professional development about formative assessment can make us better teachers. Make a case to administrators for a deep dive into the topic. Here's your pitch, courtesy of Dylan Wiliam: "An analysis of the research reveals that helping teachers develop minute-by-minute and day-by-day formative assessment practices is more cost-effective than any other strategy" (2007, p. 184).

Conclusion

Though teachers learn about formative assessment in their preservice programs, far too many misunderstand the practice, believing it is something that can be scheduled periodically or taken care of by the occasional "Does everybody understand?" But real formative assessment—the kind that can actually benefit both students and teachers enormously—is not scheduled but built in to occur throughout every lesson. Unlike summative assessments, which are administered at the end of a particular learning cycle, formative assessment provides ongoing feedback that teachers can use to improve their instruction. In fact, *decades of research surrounding formative assessment lead us to believe that there is no better way to accelerate student growth.*

5

Standardized Test-Based Practices

I'm just one stomach flu away from my goal weight.

The Devil Wears Prada, 2006

Although most educators would agree that the emphasis on high-stakes testing during the early 2000s marked a low point in our educational history, we've taken little time to remove some of the residual instructional practices that existed largely for the purposes of preparing for these high-stakes tests. We also too rarely stop to ask ourselves whether or not the actions we take in our classrooms actually support the learning and the attitudes that we truly hope to see. Are the ways in which we're gauging "success" appropriate ways to evaluate progress toward the outcomes we value the most?

In his 2009 ASCD book *Catching Up or Leading the Way,* Yong Zhao reminds U.S. educators of the dangers of undermining our strengths by trading them in for the illusion of academic progress. Born and raised in China, Zhao explains how some other countries embrace the very practices and outcomes that American educators appear so determined to throw away. In the midst of the shortsighted rush toward the implementation of No Child Left Behind (NCLB), Zhao warned that "American education is at a crossroads. We have two choices. We can destroy our strengths in order to catch up with others on test scores, or we can build on our strengths and remain a leader in innovation and creativity" (quoted in Richardson, 2009/2010, p. 20). Although we've come a long way from the self-inflicted harm that characterized much of the NCLB years, its effects on educators linger, most potently in the form of standardized test–based classroom practices that involve abandoning sound instruction and meaningful and lasting learning in order to focus on achieving higher test scores.

What's Problematic About Standardized Test–Based Practices?

The problems with standardized test–based practices can be summed up as the prioritization of the short-term appearance of progress over *actual* progress. It is time to critically analyze some of the practices that emerged during the standardization era—things like publicly displayed data walls, rigid pacing guides, teaching to the test samplers, shortchanging science and social studies, and ignoring the input of content experts—that have been normalized over the past 20 years but that actually undermine efforts toward long-term and worthwhile student learning.

This work begins with a history lesson.

Was the Nation Really at Risk?

When we ask our college students if they have heard of *A Nation at Risk* (Gardner, 1983), inevitably many hands will go up. But when we say, "Keep your hands up if you know why it is important," most of those hands will go back down. Chances are that you learned about the publication early in your education courses—one among numerous historical documents or trends that were included in your foundational curriculum.

The reason *A Nation at Risk* matters is that, practically speaking, it was one of the first government-sanctioned publications to call into question school quality and teacher credibility. It is very likely one of the main culprits in why we ever began "teaching to the test." In short, *A Nation at Risk* was commissioned by the Reagan administration as a result of the secretary of education's "concern about 'the widespread public perception that something is seriously remiss in our educational system.'" (Gardner, 1983, p. 1). The report was severe in its presentation, likening the supposedly dismal state of U.S. education to a national security threat. "If an unfriendly foreign power had attempted to impose on America the mediocre educational performance that exists today," the report intoned, "we might well have viewed it as an act of war" (p. 5). How's that for drama? *A Nation at Risk* scared readers into thinking that the United States was on the verge of losing its place as a world power. The vast majority of its pronouncements were based on the results of standardized test scores, and particularly on those that compared U.S. student achievement results with student achievement in other countries.

The Era of High-Stakes Testing—and standardization—had arrived, and with it came a serious challenge to teacher discretion.

A Flawed Premise Leads to Flawed Practice

Old as it is, *A Nation at Risk* still carries inordinate weight. While some recognize and challenge issues within the report, others reference it as if its pronouncements are beyond reproach. "We have overly criticized our schools and *A Nation at Risk* began that pattern," notes Linda Darling-Hammond (Sanchez, 2013). In contrast, former secretary of education Betsy DeVos cited the report as the beginning of a long quest for improvement that has yet to be fulfilled. Michael Petrilli, president of the Thomas B. Fordham Institute, states that the "reason that we continue to mark the anniversary is that [the content of *A Nation at Risk*] still rings true" (cited in Kamenetz, 2018).

But Anya Kamenetz (2018) interviewed two of the original writers of *A Nation at Risk*, who indicated that they were predisposed toward finding what Kamenetz calls "facts to fit the narrative." She goes on to note that "while their report is still widely cited, a second official federal government analysis of standardized test scores, produced just seven years later, showed the opposite of what was claimed in *A Nation at Risk*. That analysis found, instead, 'steady or slightly improving trends' in student achievement. The looming disaster depicted in *A Nation at Risk*, it turns out, was a matter of interpretation." Apparently, breaking up the standardized scores analyzed in the report by subgroups actually showed improvement. Moreover, the report, and much of the legislation it has inspired, was so focused on analyzing what U.S. educators did wrong that it failed to analyze what we did—and currently do—right (Zhao, 2015). The report's gloomy pronouncements never materialized. For decades after its release, the United States continued to lead the world in producing groundbreaking technology and scholarship, even surpassing nations with historically better test scores.

More than 30 years after the publication of *A Nation at Risk,* standardized test scores have not improved much. Kamenetz points to decreased funding, decreased teacher pay, and increased poverty as factors. In her view, we ought to be proud that scores haven't dropped precipitously: "In the context of declining resources and rising child poverty, maintaining steady or slightly improving test scores over decades could be described with other words besides 'flat' and 'disappointing'—perhaps 'surprising' or 'heroic'" (Kamenetz, 2018). For too long, we have assumed that we are on the verge of a national collapse when, in reality, the nation was never *really* at risk.

The Legislative Legacy

The fears sparked by *A Nation at Risk* found their crescendo in the landmark No Child Left Behind legislation. If you started teaching after 2001, the year NCLB was enacted, you may not even realize the degree to which your school's daily experiences, curricular decisions, and reliance on standardized testing have been shaped by this bill. For most of us, whether we experienced much of our K–12 schooling under NCLB or experienced much of our teaching careers under its mandates, a heavy emphasis on state standardized testing is all we've ever known. Even as NCLB recedes into the past, the damage it caused continues today.

The Tyranny of Testing . . . and Its Consequences

While it is true that purposeful classroom tests can be helpful for learning when teachers use the results to inform instruction (Boser, 2019; Hattie, 2009; Popham, 2019;), state standardized tests, which are highly susceptible to manipulation, have played a major role in the corruption of teaching in many schools and classrooms. State standardized tests were supposed to help schools keep track of inequities—and they did do that. But the results of these tests ought to have led us to providing students, particularly our most vulnerable students, with better learning opportunities, not worse.

Reasonable arguments can be made in support of some standardized tests, such as the National Assessment for Educational Progress (NAEP) assessments, which Daniel Koretz (2017) refers to as "audit tests." The NAEP results can help us to better understand where states stand in relation to one another, as well as provide data on national academic trends and progress. Under NCLB, illusions of growth on state standardized tests proliferated, but when state scores were compared against NAEP scores, which are harder to manipulate, growth was shown to be only a fraction of what districts and states had reported. (One example of this disparity can be seen in the yearly gains on standardized test scores that New York City schools reported under NCLB but that were not reflected in NAEP results; see Koretz, 2017.) Additionally, state standardized test score increases in elementary schools do not appear to be sustained in middle and high schools, particularly when the middle schools exist as their own separate entities (West & Schwerdt, 2012; Wexler, 2019).

Across the country, there is little evidence that NCLB-inspired test-based instruction has had any lasting effect. According to Monty Neill, the executive director of FairTest (quoted in Strauss, 2015), scores on the SAT, ACT, and PISA (Programme for International Student Assessment) either declined or flattened while NCLB was in effect (2003–2013). More recent results from 2019 show that in all three tested grade clusters—4th, 8th, and 12th—NAEP reading scores remained flat or were lower than scores on pre-NCLB assessments from 1998. In fact, the latest comparisons show that the gap between high and low performers is widening (Ravitch, 2020). For educators who lived through the most stringent years of NCLB, this prompts a question: what did we gain for all of our attempts to improve state scores? Likewise, and of equal importance, what did we lose?

Similar to extreme and harmful fad diets that are focused only on outward appearances, the task of raising test scores is not so hard to do when teaching is laser-focused on only those skills that are covered by the tests. But higher test scores on one test do not necessarily translate into long-term academic improvement. For example, here's Koretz (2017) describing math score increases that fizzled over time: "The best estimate is that test-based accountability may have produced modest gains in elementary-school mathematics but no appreciable gains in either reading or high-school mathematics—even though reading and mathematics have been its primary focus" (p. 6).

Worst yet, modest increases in scores lead schools to fall further into the test-prep trap. Alfie Kohn (2006a) posits that those who argue for standardized testing use circular reasoning to assert that a focus on testing will raise standardized test scores: "Consider the inconsistent insistence on 'scientifically validated' or research-based' education policies.... Indeed the only data ever cited in defense of high-stakes testing consist of higher scores on the same tests that are used to enforce this agenda. Apart from the inherent methodological problems this raises, the fact is that scores can be made to rise even though meaningful learning, as assessed in other ways, does not improve at all" (p. 11).

John Hattie (2009) reviewed several meta-analyses that attempted to measure the effectiveness of standardized testing. His analysis provided mixed results that are far from convincing. Research also shows that classroom practices focused on test scores have grave costs in terms of learning opportunities and time spent on things that matter (Kohn, 2015; Koretz, 2017). A teacher focused on increasing state test scores will likely see those scores temporarily increase, but the toll on meaningful learning may be immense. Here's Kohn again: "The reality is that these tests mostly serve to make dreadful teaching appear successful" (quoted in Strauss, 2019). Kohn also notes the uncomfortable truth that high standardized test scores are more reflective of zip codes than of any other student characteristics.

Positive Alternatives to Standardized Test-Based Practices

Unlike prior chapters, in this one we've folded the research that supports our "this is problematic" argument into the presentation of positive alternatives. And in some cases, the positive alternative is simply to refrain from implementing the problematic practice. We know that many decisions about standardized testing are beyond the scope of individual teachers, so we've made sure to stick with ideas that are within teachers' areas of influence and the actions they can take in their own classrooms.

Maintain Healthy Skepticism Toward Data-Driven Decision Making

At first glance, data-driven decision making seems to make perfect sense: identify students who need support and provide them with the support they need. How could anyone not want to keep close tabs on student progress so that they can more adequately target their instruction? "But data-driven reforms often encourage educators to go further than this," writes Shanahan (2014). "They champion the idea that item analysis of standardized tests will allow teachers to know not only who may be having trouble but also which skills these students lack" (p. 184). The result? Intensively pointed instructional sessions that focus entirely on literacy skill development and are devoid of any meaningful experiences with books.

Too often, we think of literacy as being composed of discrete skills that can be taught and assessed at specific points in time and in isolation one from the other. But assessing these skills in isolation doesn't tell us whether a child can or cannot apply them as a reader, writer, or learner. In discussing a teacher who was knee-deep in data-driven school reform, Shanahan (2014) writes: "Her plan was to give kids lots of practice answering test questions of particular types. The problem with such a plan is that it doesn't actually work. As you've seen, students may fail to answer particular questions, but not because they can't execute those skills. Giving students a lot of practice with those kinds of test items is not likely to improve achievement at all. It could even lower it, since there are better things that students could be doing to prepare for such testing" (p. 187).

Hamilton and colleagues (2009) found only minimal evidence that data-driven decision making actually works. Mike Schmoker (2018) points out that "such test-preparation exertions sometimes have a slight upward effect on scores, but then the scores plateau" (p. 37). Harvard professor Heather Hill eloquently sums up the process of analyzing student assessment data in this way: "Understanding students' weaknesses is only useful if it changes practice. And, to date, evidence suggests that it does not change practice—or student outcomes. Focusing on the problem has likely distracted us from focusing on the solution" (Hill, 2020, para. 4).

Data-driven school reform has led to an overwhelmingly simplified and decontextualized emphasis on skill development at the expense of time spent reading, talking about reading, and writing about reading. It is perfectly commendable to try to understand students' strengths and areas of need for the purpose of offering strategically targeted instruction. But when we shoot for isolated, laser-focused, item-analysis-crazed, data-driven school reform, we can easily forget that reading is a complex process involving components that cannot be easily measured in isolation. Instead, let's evaluate how connected our teaching is to the larger goal of raising competent and thriving readers. Let's invest more in actions that lead us toward that larger goal: time in class spent reading, talking about reading, and writing about reading.

Take Down the Data Walls (Keep Progress Private)

If you do an internet search for "classroom data walls," you'll find colorful displays (often green, yellow, and red) containing rows or columns identifying areas of content mastery. Look closer, and you'll often see students' names affixed to color-coded designations identifying each student's performance on each assessed skill. In an effort to provide students with anonymity, some data walls contain student-assigned numbers instead of names, although it is not difficult for peers to quickly decipher who is in the red. These public displays of progress, heavily emphasized during the NCLB era, persist in many of today's schools and classrooms. Data walls are a means of progress monitoring, but their public nature is intended to motivate students to work toward a goal of moving out of the red and into the yellow, or out of the yellow and into the green.

Setting up and maintaining data walls is not just a significant drain on teacher's time, it's arguably a total waste of it. This is because research does not support data walls as an effective way to support student success (Hill, 2020; Koretz, 2017; Schmoker, 2018). And in a systematic review of 30 empirical studies focusing on data walls, Harris and colleagues (2020) found that although teachers and researchers tend to argue in favor of the practice, student voices (when included at all) were more negative.

We have seen data walls hung in the back of classrooms that clearly displayed the winners and the losers in the quest toward math and reading skills mastery. Additionally, these types of checklists, complete with directions for gimmicks and incentives, now flood the pages of websites like Pinterest and Teachers Pay Teachers. Publicly displayed data walls visually stratify students according to their test scores. Imagine the impact this has on students who consistently see their progress in the red zones. Imagine the impact on English learners, students with special needs, and students who are struggling to learn. Think about what it would be like to feel that all your peers see your progress and shake their heads in dismay. Most of the studies reviewed by Harris and colleagues (2020) raised concerns about the negative impact of data walls on student motivation, and at least one study records instances where students who were in "the red zone," the lowest achievers, were "mocked or derided" by their peers. In fact, it is likely that the only type of students who like data walls are the ones that are consistently in the green.

Public praise and shaming aren't limited to data walls. One middle school we visited rewarded students by placing motivational paper cutouts on the lockers of students who had performed well on interim tests. Though the intent was benign, the result was a sort of badge of shame in reverse, since lower achievers were left with conspicuously bare lockers. And the same concerns we mention here about data walls also apply to public charts showing teachers' classroom outcomes hung in hallways and faculty lounges. What impact do we suppose these charts have on teachers? At least two studies have found that charts comparing teacher performance seemed to undermine teacher motivation (Harris et al., 2020).

The solution to this problematic practice is simple: for the sake of creating a culture of learning that is motivating, that is compassionate, and that fosters collaboration toward everyone's growth, keep student and teacher data private.

Prioritize Curricular Depth over Breadth

Many universities offer what are derisively known as "DFW" courses, where a large proportion of students either earn *D*s or *F*s or end up withdrawing. We'd love to say that DFW courses are limited to higher education, but they exist in K–12 schools, too.

Many of the suggested solutions for reducing the number of DFW courses in universities are the same things that work in K–12 classrooms, mainly that of placing an intentional focus on student learning. And as it turns out, when we place the focus on student learning, the teaching consequentially improves. Here's how Wiggins and McTighe (2005) put it: "Teaching, on its own, never causes learning. Only successful attempts by the learner to learn cause learning. Achievement is the result of the learner successfully making sense of the teaching" (p. 228). You can teach all you want, as intensely as you can, but unless a student is actively making sense of the content, you can't expect that student to learn.

Meaningful and lasting learning is most likely to occur when we slow down and design experiences that require students to deeply process big ideas in our curriculum. "Given the unobvious, often counterintuitive, and otherwise abstract nature of big ideas, the understandings have to be 'earned' through carefully designed experiences that uncover the possible meanings of core content," write Wiggins and McTighe (2005). "Few textbooks are designed around a series of defining experiences, yet well-designed experience is the only way to make ideas real" (p. 233). We can easily help to ensure student learning by embedding opportunities to read, write, and talk about content in every lesson. As Mike Schmoker (2018) notes, "To optimize and enliven learning, our curriculum must be liberally infused with frequent opportunities for students to read, discuss, argue, and write about what they are learning" (p. 28).

Structured student talk

Well-designed opportunities to increase student talk can go a long way toward supporting deep learning. We say "well-designed" because student talk can lead to greater learning, but it can also undermine learning if opportunities for student talk are not carefully designed with purposeful prompts, unambiguous directions, and clear expected outcomes. To design such learning opportunities, take time to develop purposeful stopping points and related prompts and to support content-focused discussions where students can articulate their own understandings and make their learning strategies "visible" to one other (Murata et al., 2017).

A meta-analysis reviewing 71 studies on peer interaction and student talk concluded that although interacting with an adult was better than interacting with student peers, at any age, well-structured student-to-student interactions had a positive effect on learning (Tenenbaum et al., 2019). The greatest benefits were observed when teachers provided structure and explicit instructions on what to do while students were talking (e.g., requiring them to achieve consensus on a certain issue). "Our findings indicate that the benefits of peer interaction can be realized by educators if they create opportunities not just for discussion, but also for the negotiation of a shared understanding," the researchers conclude (p. 14).

Student writing

There is something about writing—the organization and written expression of one's knowledge—that furthers student learning. Graham and colleagues (2020) reviewed 56 studies and found that, in most of them, writing about content enhanced student learning across content areas and grade levels. Another meta-analysis by Graham and Hebert (2010) showed "that having students write about the material they read does enhance their reading abilities. In fact, 57 out of 61 outcomes (93 percent) were positive, indicating a consistent and positive effect for writing about what is read" (p. 13). These results were consistent across grades 2 through 12; across science, social studies, and English language arts; and across achievement levels. "Writing about a text proved to be better than just reading it, reading and rereading it, reading and studying it, reading and discussing it, and receiving reading instruction" (p. 14).

Restructuring and reducing the standards

"Standards are necessary, and having them has made me a better teacher," writes teacher and author Kelly Gallagher (2009). "However, there is one big problem concerning the state and local standards in this country: there are too many of them. Is it just me, or would it take weeks to teach any one of the preceding standards with any depth?" (p. 9). Teaching for depth requires that we combine, reorganize, and restructure standards to make them more manageable. "Once the standards are reduced and revised," writes Schmoker (2018), "any willing team of teachers can produce a curriculum that is superior to what prevails in the majority of schools" (p. 45).

Don't Be Bullied by a Rigid Pacing Guide

A pacing guide is a schedule of intended action items and goals that teachers use to structure a given year or learning cycle. They can be written in general terms with "suggested" time frames, or they can be rigidly prescribed, right down to dictating the textbook pages students should read each day. While pacing guides can serve as helpful road maps, if they are too rigid, they can eat away at teacher discretion and keep them from structuring their classes in ways that work for their students. In the words of Sir Ken Robinson (2013), "If you remove teachers' discretion, it stops working."

Pacing guides can cause particular challenges for teaching English learners. We have seen teachers in linguistically diverse classrooms struggle to justify barreling through curriculum at a frenetic pace despite their students not understanding the content. In one class we visited with a high number of English learners, district administrators would make pop-in visits to make sure that teachers were strictly following the pacing guide. "It just feels wrong," one teacher told us. "I thought that we were the experts!" said another. "The fact that we're terrified of saying that we need an extra week means that we are not advocating for what kids need." Pacing guides assume a degree of uniformity among learners that simply doesn't exist. For them to work as intended, all students would have to progress at the same rate and function at the same levels, year after year. In addition, the guides don't allow for "getting lost in the learning" or for teachers to exploit teachable moments.

Guardrails can be helpful, but nobody appreciates or is helped by a backseat driver. Likewise, when the pacing guide stops feeling like a guide and starts feeling like handcuffs, it has gone too far. When it specifically tells us what we should be teaching, down to the exact day, it removes teacher discretion and has gone too far. When it requires blind obedience and fidelity to a flawed curriculum, it has gone too far. When it leaves no time for reading, writing, and discussing, and when it calls for surface-level learning of important concepts resulting in little actual learning, it has gone too far. When it causes us to ignore the needs of our English learners, our learners experiencing trauma, our students with special needs, and our most vulnerable students, it is time to draw the line. The pacing guide has gone too far.

Teachers, let's trust ourselves and our professional training and teach in ways that will serve every student in our care. If this requires advocacy, then let's get together and advocate. Our students are worth it.

Resist Teaching to the Test Samplers

The content of state standardized tests is rarely a surprise. In an effort to support schools in putting their best foot forward, states will provide schools with "test samplers," or examples of "eligible content," delineating what will be on the test. The problem comes when we focus so heavily on the samplers that we ignore the rest of the content that surrounds the larger domain. We previously touched upon the problems inherent with "teaching to the test." Koretz (2017) sums up a big part of it this way:

> If you teach a domain [well]—say, geometry—scores on a good test of that area will go up. However, if you directly teach the small sample measured by a particular test—for example, memorization of the fact that vertical angles are equal—scores will increase, often dramatically, but mastery of geometry as a whole will not improve much, if at all. (p. 18)

And, of course, these increases will be short-lived. The test samplers that teachers receive from test publishers and from their state departments of education are woefully inadequate for helping students develop a deep understanding of content. "Test-based accountability has led to a corruption of the ideals of teaching," writes Koretz (2017, p. 6). As hard as it is, we have to force ourselves to resist the temptation to teach to the samplers and, instead, to meaningfully teach the domain that the sampler is supposed to represent. We understand that this may be too much to ask for many who serve in districts where high-stakes testing is emphasized. If this is you, we advise trying to limit the test prep to a few isolated sessions close to standardized testing time. Don't allow this emphasis to overwhelm your teaching.

To prepare students for standardized tests without narrowing the curriculum, Shanahan (2014) suggests that teachers do the following:

- Give students time to read extensively within instruction.
- Provide students with opportunities to read without guidance.
- Supply students with texts that are sufficiently challenging and rich in content.
- Have students provide text-based responses to prompts.
- Ask students to write about what they read.

In other words, if you want students to both learn well and do well on standardized tests, they will need lots of time to *actually engage in reading*—with teacher guidance, with one another, and on their own. Schmoker (2018), too, repeatedly reminds teachers to give students opportunities to read, discuss, and write. For English learners especially, we have found that there simply is no substitute to the three components of reading, writing, and talking about learning.

Though teaching to the test samplers may provide a temporary increase in scores, the perceived growth will typically not persist, and it will not transfer to nontest formats or to audit tests measuring the same (but larger) domain. "It is much as though a campaign tried to win an election by convincing the 800 polled people—and only those 800 people—to vote for their candidate," writes Koretz (2017, p. 18). Instead, let's teach the larger domain so well that the samplers will be understood by default. Let's focus on meaningful learning where we engage students in content not because we think it will appear on a test, but because the content matters.

Reprioritize a Love of Reading

Being able to foster in students an interest in and a love of reading will support almost every other educational aim we have. But helping students develop a love for reading was a widespread casualty of the Era of High-Stakes Testing. Not only do children today read less than those in years past, but as they transition from 2nd to 3rd grade, their interest in reading drops dramatically: 40 percent of 8-year-olds report that they love reading, as compared to only 28 percent of 9-year-olds (Scholastic, 2019). We get it. We asked our 3rd grade daughter how she felt about reading. (Note that this was her first year experiencing state standardized testing.) Her response was telling: "I love to read, but I hate *learning* to read."

Kelly Gallagher (2009) would refer to what happened to our daughter and those 9-year-olds as "readicide"—"the systematic killing of the love of reading, often exacerbated by the inane, mind-numbing practices found in schools" (p. 2). According to Gallagher, much of the blame is due to our obsession with raising standardized test scores. Today, long after the height of NCLB, commercial core reading programs and their supplemental worksheets still dictate how students spend their reading time. Students spend little quality time actually *reading,* and the reading levels of the books they're assigned are far beyond many students' ability.

The International Literacy Association (ILA) is clear: "Two powerful instructional practices—teacher-led read-alouds and in-school independent reading—have the power and promise to set students on a path of lifelong reading" (ILA, 2018, p.2). Read-alouds also address the issue of equity; as Allington (2014) notes, "It is children from low-income families that routinely lack access to books. They rarely have home libraries of books" (p. 21). For these students, time spent reading and classroom read-alouds can make all the difference.

First among the seven core values of the National Council of Teachers of English (NCTE) is this: "As English language arts teachers, we provide protected opportunities within our classrooms that allow students to increase their volume of reading through independent reading of self-selected texts" (2019, para. 8). Unfortunately, commercial basal readers alone do a poor job of capturing students' attention. One basal reader used in a classroom we visited had students spend a week reading a short excerpt from one of our favorite middle grade children's books, but the story fell flat. The selected excerpt required a great deal of backstory in the novel. And this backstory was absent in the isolated excerpt that had been plucked out of the book. While this was a well-meaning attempt to expose students to characterization through an excellent story, the folks behind the basal reader failed to realize that truly understanding characterization requires immersion, not just a snippet. Learning to like a character takes time.

One of the biggest problems with classrooms focused on increasing test scores is that students are given little in-school time to enjoy the read-aloud, little opportunity to choose what they read, and little time to read self-selected books. Time spent reading and the ability to choose what is read are important, research-backed practices that build motivation to read as well as proficiency in reading (Gambrell, 2011). Additionally, researchers point to a direct correlation between students' exposure to books, their time spent reading, and their schooling outcomes (Allington, 2011; Cunningham, 2001; ILA, 2018; Krashen, 2004). Though the National Reading Panel (2000) questioned the effectiveness of sustained silent reading as an instructional tool, numerous researchers dispute their recommendations (see Allington, 2011; Cunningham, 2001; Edmondson & Shannon, 2002; Garan & DeVoogd, 2008; Krashen, 2005; Sanden, 2014). There are hundreds of studies that draw correlations between the amount of time spent reading and reading achievement (Garan & DeVoogd, 2008). We discussed this topic in more detail in Chapter 3.

Building habitual readers is important. What reading teachers do is more than simply teaching children the mechanics of how to read. And reading is more than a skill; it is a tool for discovering so much else. If we expect students to love reading enough to want to do it, enough to see real increases in reading abilities, we need to prioritize allowing students to get lost in the pages of a good book, right within our classrooms.

In an effort to establish a community of readers who regularly read books, talked about books, analyzed books, and enjoyed a healthy dose of read-alouds, Pérsida implemented the use of a "classroom bookworm" in her 6th grade classroom. And to demonstrate a love for reading, and that reading happens at all ages, during sustained silent reading time, Pérsida read a book of her own. Each time a student finished a book, they had the choice of completing an optional book review like the one in Figure 5.1 and affixing it to a construction-paper "bookworm" that Pérsida had placed above the classroom door (see Figure 5.2). Before adding their segment, students shared their reviews with the rest of the class, often resulting in students calling dibs on reading that book next.

Although the book reviews were optional, by the end of the year, the bookworm had grown to zigzag around the entire room, with the tail meeting the head. The class averaged 10 voluntary book reviews per student. And for the few students who did not elect to write book reviews,

Pérsida made a point of adding extra individual reading conferences to effectively monitor their reading habits without subjecting them to what would have felt like forced drudgery.

Figure 5.1 Bookworm Review Template

Bookworm review by: ______________________ Date: ____________

Title and author:

Without giving away the ending, give us a feel for what the book is about.

Give us some feedback about this book. What's on your heart?

Briefly talk about the genre; talk about who would, or would not, like the book.

Source: From *Total Literacy Techniques: Tools to Help Students Analyze Literature and Informational Texts* (p. 79), by P. Himmele and W. Himmele with K. Potter, 2014, Alexandria, VA: ASCD. Copyright 2014 by ASCD.

Figure 5.2 Classroom Bookworm

Recenter Social Studies and Sciences as Essential Disciplines

The standardized testing obsession of NCLB led schools to deemphasize science and social studies. Yet when we ask teachers to list the outcome they desire most for graduates, "being a productive and informed citizen" is often at the top of the list. We need a population of critical thinkers who are equipped to analyze human interdependence and global interconnectivity. When we travel abroad, we are always surprised at how much foreigners know about U.S. history—and how little Americans know about theirs. The social sciences matter. But because they have not been the focus of high-stakes tests, they have received less attention in our schools.

In grades 1 through 5, students spend less time in science and social studies than they do on any other subject areas, including noncore subjects. While elementary students spend approximately two hours on English language arts and 80 minutes on math daily, they spend 30 minutes or less a day on science and social studies (Tyner & Kabourek, 2020). Any elementary school teacher who has taught science well knows that 30 minutes is hardly enough time to do the type of science that engages students and allows them to develop conceptual understandings of content.

Additionally, Tyner and Kabourek (2020) found that those who received an additional 30 minutes of social studies instruction per day improved their reading more quickly than students who did not. "Our findings imply that shifting 20, 30, or even 40 minutes away from less effective ELA activities (such as practicing comprehension skills) and reinvesting that time to learn more about geography, history, civics, and the like will improve students' reading ability," write the authors (p. 29). What's more, the benefits of social studies instruction on reading ability were especially acute for students from lower socioeconomic backgrounds. "Instead of devoting more class time to English language arts (ELA)," write Tyner and Kabourek (2020), "we should be teaching elementary school children more social studies—as in, rich content about history, geography, and civics. That may seem counterintuitive, but that's the key takeaway of this groundbreaking study" (p. 1). If we truly value a "productive and informed citizenry," then we need to make room for social studies.

According to the National Science Teaching Association (NSTA), great science teaching aims to "involve students in scientific discourse to help them make evidence-based conclusions and decisions, and communicate those conclusions and decisions effectively through speaking and writing" (NSTA, 2018, para. 7). Science is just too important to ignore. It's already on the state standards; we just need to commit to actually teaching it. If this is an area in which you feel you need professional development (PD), don't be afraid to ask for it. Specify that you're interested in PD that focuses on the teaching of hands-on, minds-on science. You might also want to check out the resources that already exist for you on NSTA.org.

Teachers, let's evaluate what we make time for in our classrooms. We're preparing the world's future scientists, politicians, teachers, leaders, and informed citizens. We risk limiting exposure to these important fields to students from families already immersed in these practices. If students don't get inspired within our classrooms, where will they get inspired? Let's make time in our teaching for the things that matter and for the things we say we value.

Listen to the Content Experts

The failure of big-named professional organizations to rally behind high-stakes accountability in schools ought to have been a warning to states' departments of education. If there were going to be a national emphasis on increasing accountability for the teaching and learning of reading and math, you'd think you'd want the National Council of Teachers of Mathematics (NCTM), the International Literacy Association (ILA), and the National Council of Teachers of English (NCTE) behind you. Yet position papers publicly posted by these groups show uniform opposition to states' unhealthy emphasis on standardized test–based accountability.

NCTM warns that standardized test scores can be overanalyzed and lead to invalid inferences. It favors instead basing instructional decisions on multiple sources of information and especially on in-class formative assessments (NCTM, 2016). NCTE doesn't pull any punches in its rebuke of "large-scale, standardized, high-stakes literacy assessments, especially normative tests," which, it argues, "can distort student development and achievement: often, they are misaligned with literacy standards and/

or with a given school's curricular outcomes. In addition, they are often misused: although they are not designed for diagnostic purposes, they are often used for such purposes, thus violating an important principle of literacy assessment regarding purposefulness" (NCTE, 2018, para. 11). In fact, NCTE has been ringing alarm bells since long before NCLB existed. Here is a statement the organization issued way back in 1995: "NCTE has repeatedly warned that a preoccupation with large-scale standardized testing leads to distortion and reduction of this curriculum and to unwise expenditure of public funds that could be better spent on teaching programs" (para. 2). And in 1999, ILA (then the International Reading Association) stated plainly that it was opposed to high-stakes testing.

Generally speaking, when you feel as though you can't get a straight answer about a major occurrence within a specific field of study—you are hearing one thing from your content area leaders, another from your school administrators, and yet another from a magazine article you read—head to the websites of professional organizations like the ones we've mentioned here and see what they have to say. These organizations are not connected to policymakers or state departments of education, and they don't have any partisan or political mandates or agendas to uphold. Instead, they represent the brightest minds in their content areas, who have consolidated their thoughts into position statements and resources that you can often access easily for free. When in doubt, check with the experts.

Conclusion

Much has changed since NCLB was the order of the day, but there are still related issues that we need to address. Excellent instruction involves helping students develop big-picture understandings of historical and scientific content, deeply analyze literature, and make sense of complex mathematics and other content—none of which can be adequately taught using practices designed to raise scores on standardized tests. Yong Zhao puts it succinctly: "Why would you want to abandon great art programs, music programs, science programs, technology programs, sports programs, so we can focus on learning that can occur basically by memorizing from a book?" (in Richardson, 2009/2010, p. 20). We need to challenge practices that don't reflect what we value most and what we know about student learning. It's long past time that we shed the remnants of No Child Left Behind and embrace learning that is deep and enduring.

6

Behavior Charts and Withholding Recess

I do not like the cone of shame.
Up, 2009

A punitive response to student misconduct can often feel like the most effective and logical consequence to student misbehaviors, but in reality, when it involves shame, it often leads to repeated or worse behaviors (Cassiello-Robbins et al., 2019; Reinke et al., 2016; Simonton & Garn, 2020; Sommer et al., 2020). Such is the case with behavior charts and other behavior management strategies that unintentionally shame students. Likewise, although withholding recess from students will immediately result in downcast expressions and instant regret, it also leads to other outcomes that can exacerbate problematic behaviors and end up doing more harm than good.

What's Problematic About Behavior Charts and Withholding Recess?

Behavior charts and losing recess may serve as short-term deterrents to certain disruptive or harmful behaviors, but as we'll highlight in the following sections, research points to evidence that both are likely to have more lasting negative effects than positive ones. Behavior charts and withholding recess do little to repair the harm caused by students deviating from classroom expectations. Nor do they factor in personal growth for students.

Let's look now at why these persistent practices generally end up doing more harm than good.

Behavior Charts as Public Shaming

Behavior charts are public displays of students' behavioral status in class, and they're used primarily in the elementary grades. A kind of behavior chart that's common in today's classrooms is an arrangement of pockets that resembles a shoe organizer. There is a pocket for each student in the classroom, and each student's pocket has his or her name on it and contains a stack of color-coded cards that can be reordered to reflect that student's "current behavior." Another common behavior chart format features movable name clips or clothespins. When students commit an infraction, the teacher will direct them to "pull a color" or "change your clip." Though the intent is to curb disruptive behavior, behavior charts will often inadvertently shame students and do little to teach positive behavior.

Teachers who use behavior charts quickly realize that it's usually the same students who keep "pulling colors" over and over again, and this fact alone ought to cause us to question the approach's effectiveness. We can expect that students who are faced with constant defeat will eventually stop trying to change their behaviors. Worse yet, they may become comfortable with their disruptive persona. For these children, the behavior chart may be less a deterrent than a self-fulfilling prophecy (Kowalski & Froiland, 2020; Reinke et al., 2016; Simonton & Garn, 2020).

In addition to getting a little too comfortable with their role as "bad kids," students who repeatedly appear on the behavior chart can easily learn how to rig the system. Our son once told us that he had no idea what would happen if a child pulled three cards, because every child in his class stopped at two. Day after day, he told us, he pulled exactly two cards, knowing that the third would lead to an awful penalty—although what exactly this penalty was, he couldn't say, because no one ever actually experienced it.

Asking students to pull a card or change their clip doesn't help them learn how to behave, let alone develop the skills they need to thrive as positive members of the classroom community. Think, too, of the constant interruptions to lessons that behavior charts present, as teachers must regularly call on students to change their card or clip. In these instances, both the teacher and the students lose their focus on learning.

Furthermore, whether intended or not, behavior charts function as a form of public shaming. As Jung and Smith (2018) remind us, "Nowhere in the literature do researchers recommend that we shame children into being compliant" (p. 15). Katie Hurley (2016), a psychotherapist and parent educator, describes the perils of behavior charts well:

> I get a lot of phone calls from parents desperate to help their kids stop worrying so much about the academic and behavioral demands they face at school each day. Is it the actual chart that causes the anxiety? No, more often than not it's the fear of being ridiculed by peers or disappointing or upsetting the teacher and/or the parent that triggers stress and anxiety. Being judged in a public way, all day, every day, makes it difficult to enjoy learning. (para. 8)

Parenting expert Wendy Thomas Russell (2016) describes a kindergarten student's empathy for classmates who experienced the shame of the behavior chart. This student also experienced overwhelming anxiety over the predicament of ever having her color changed. "And then it happened," Russell writes. "The teacher moved the girl's color from green down to yellow. [She] came home and told her parents she wanted to kill herself. She was 5" (paras. 7–8). Shaming children doesn't further the goal of community building, but rather actively tears it down. "The fact of the matter is, when we use behavior charts, we are sacrificing student dignity in favor of teacher convenience," write Jung and Smith (2018, p. 16).

According to Amanda Harmon Cooley (2018), "School shaming punishments result in extraordinary and enduring harm for both the penalized student and the school community" (p. 340). Indeed, the practice of shaming students has been linked to an increase in negative outcomes like anger, school violence, and self-destructive behaviors (Cassiello-Robbins et al., 2019; Sommer et al., 2020). For highly sensitive children who are not prone to outbursts, shaming can also lead to high levels of anxiety that inhibit learning. Children who experience shame experience a spike in cortisol that can remain elevated for 40 minutes, and elevated cortisol has been shown to have a negative effect on students' self-image and ability to learn (Lewis & Ramsay, 2002; Mills et al., 2008).

Children are, by nature, energetic, fun-loving, and active. Hurley (2016) reminds us that "kids are wiggly, easily distracted and quick to excitement because they're young, not because they're poorly behaved. When kids face the same behavioral intervention over and over again, they begin to develop negative core beliefs. Instead of thinking, 'I'm having a hard day,' they tend to think, 'I'm a bad kid and no one likes me.'" Oddly enough, some of the very traits we try to suppress in school are highly valued in adulthood. For example, talkativeness can be seen as gregariousness, or stubbornness as persistence. Many of those children who are always "fooling around" make delightful co-workers when they grow up. It's important that we help students understand that these are not bad characteristics; they are actually highly valued ones. The students simply need to get better at self-regulating so that these characteristics don't interfere with their own learning or their peers' learning while in a classroom setting. It ought to concern us that some students believe they have to choose between being compliant and being interesting.

Withholding Recess

When we visit elementary schools, we'll occasionally notice, at the periphery of the recess yards full of laughing and screaming children, one or two children seated near the schoolhouse and looking deflated. Of course, sometimes students do need a time-out—when they're overly aggressive or pose some sort of safety risk to themselves or their peers, for example. But teachers will often also withhold recess as consequences for rule infractions that have nothing to do with what's happening on the playground. We believe this to be a mistake, and the research supports us.

The American Academy of Pediatrics makes a number of points in its 2013 policy statement "The Crucial Role of Recess in School." Among them are these:

- Recess is a necessary break in the day for optimizing a child's social, emotional, physical, and cognitive development. In essence, recess should be considered a child's personal time, and it should not be withheld for academic or punitive reasons.
- Cognitive processing and academic performance depend on regular breaks from concentrated classroom work. This applies equally to adolescents and to younger children. To be effective, the frequency and duration of breaks should be sufficient to allow the students to mentally decompress. (p. 186)

Parent frustrations regarding withholding recess run so deep that a Google search using "withholding recess as punishment" will turn up a long list of parent blogs and articles with personal stories of how children as young as preschoolers have been denied recess for infractions that likely pointed to a need for recess in the first place. As Rebecca London (2019) explains, "Withholding recess is counterintuitive because the students who have trouble sitting still or being quiet are often the ones who would benefit the most from some free time to move around and regain their focus" (p. 50).

In the days of NCLB, schools saw an overall decrease in recess times, particularly in response to increases in reading and math instruction time (Henley et al., 2007). And although the Every Student Succeeds Act (ESSA) does require health and physical education, it does not mandate recess or outdoor play (Stapp & Karr, 2018). Yet as Sheryl Venable (2017) articulates, recess is vital to the overall health of students: "Suppose a supervisor of adult workers decided that eliminating breaks would increase the company's productivity. Would workers accept this? They probably would not. Why then would we decrease or eliminate children's breaks? Recess periods are children's breaks from their jobs as students" (p. 75).

Researchers have found that daily recess improves academic achievement, physical health, and the ability of students to focus for extended periods in class (Hyndman & Wyver, 2020; London et al., 2015; McNamara & Walker, 2018; Stapp & Karr, 2018; Venable, 2017). It's as if children are trying to tell us, "Look, we're going to get our energy out one way or another, so you might as well work with us instead of against us."

Chang and Coward (2015) describe an Asian-American mother's surprise at the limited breaks provided for students in U.S. schools: "This parent was accustomed to the Chinese school schedule, in which students have a 10-minute recess time for every 40 minutes of instruction, excluding the lunch break and "nap time" right after lunch. . . . She simply couldn't understand why the school would expect her young son to remain focused on his lessons for the whole day when most adults are themselves unable to stay focused for even a one-hour presentation" (p. 14). If our goal is to encourage children's emotional, social, and moral development, recess is the perfect way to do it. In fact, some argue that we should also extend the length of breaks between learning periods (Chang & Coward, 2015; Pellegrini & Bjorklund, 1997; Rodríguez-Fernández et al., 2020).

Positive Alternatives to Behavior Charts and Withholding Recess

While practices like behavior charts and withholding recess are attempts to create positive classroom environments by minimizing disruptions, they do little to promote healthy behaviors. In recent years, we have seen more emphasis on social and emotional learning (SEL) as an alternative to practices that unwittingly shame students or reinforce problematic behaviors. After all, the research shows that SEL increases students' sense of belonging and overall well-being.

Although any one definition of it is undoubtedly incomplete, in general, SEL focuses on helping students develop healthy personal identities and thrive in social and academic learning contexts. "Social-emotional learning . . . involves the processes through which children and adults acquire and effectively apply the knowledge, attitudes, and skills necessary to understand and manage emotions, set and achieve positive goals, feel and show empathy for others, establish and maintain positive relationships, and make responsible decisions," write Bridgeland and colleagues (2013, p. 16).

A meta-analysis by Durlak and colleagues (2011) found that SEL programs resulted in improved mental health and social skills and an 11-percentile gain in academic performance. More recently, Taylor and colleagues (2017) found that SEL produced favorable outcomes with regard to academic performance, relationships, socioeconomic status, and mental health as well as sustained academic improvements, including an average 13-percentile academic advantage over peers who did not participate in SEL programs. Additionally, Belfield and colleagues (2015) found that SEL provided an overall benefit–cost ratio of 11:1 across six interventions. Their analysis suggests that the costs of implementing SEL are far outweighed by the returns, including things like reductions in substance abuse and other improvements in quality of life.

"[T]he promotion of social, emotional, and academic learning is not a shifting educational fad," declares the Aspen Institute (2019), but "the substance of education itself. It is not a distraction from the 'real work' of math and English instruction; it is how instruction can succeed" (p. 6). We can understand why they feel the need to remind us to address education in a more holistic manner. The evidence of the effectiveness of SEL serves to remind us all of the importance of serving the whole child and the counterintuitive nature of ignoring social and emotional aspects of learning.

Social and emotional learning addresses an essential feature of our humanity. "In schools that lift up nearly all their students, educators have learned that what makes students thrive is what makes people human—emotions," writes Brackett (2018). "When schools recognize that emotions drive much of how and what we learn, students and educators flourish" (p. 13). After the wrong turn of NCLB, when students were treated as little more than academic inputs and outputs, SEL reminds us that we cannot successfully educate students while bypassing their essential human need to be valued. Our suggested alternatives to behavior charts and withholding recess all focus on the development of SEL skills that can benefit children for the rest of their lives.

Restorative Practices

Behavior charts and withholding recess may serve as short-term deterrents to misbehavior, but their limitations are that they do little to fix the problem or to repair any harm done to classmates who may have been hurt as a result of the misconduct, nor do they address the personal growth of the student who is being punished. "In contrast," write

Acosta and colleagues (2015), "restorative school practices are based on the premise that students need to take responsibility for their actions by addressing the students they hurt" (p. 24). While a specific consequence may still be issued using restorative practices, the focus is on repairing harm and restoring dignity.

Although long evident in indigenous histories, modern restorative practices—a hallmark of SEL—find their origins in a 1974 criminal justice innovation known as the victim–offender reconciliation program. To Howard Zehr (2004), a restorative justice pioneer, wrongs are a violation of people and relationships that lead to one central obligation, which is to put right the wrongs. To this end, restorative practices involve facilitating direct conversations between the offenders and the victims. In classrooms that adopt restorative practices, the humans, not the punishment, take center stage.

Restorative practices in education address three interconnected issues:

- Creating just and equitable learning environments
- Nurturing healthy relationships
- Repairing harm and transforming conflict (Evans & Vaandering, 2016, p. 5)

Meanwhile, Smith and colleagues (2015) lay out two important components of restorative practices: relationships and high-quality instruction. "Restorative practices are predicated on the positive relationships that students and adults have with one another," they write. "Simply said, it's harder for students to act defiantly or disrespectfully toward adults who clearly care about them and their future" (p. 4). In recent years, the concepts behind restorative practices have been embraced around the country; for example, Oakland Unified offers a free guide and numerous resources to help schools adopt restorative practices at its website, www.ousd.org.

For those who would like a deeper immersion in restorative practices, we recommend the book *Better Than Carrots or Sticks* (Smith et al., 2015) as an individual read or book study. The stories it contains are moving, and it has purposeful anecdotes and practical tools to help you address short-term and long-term goals for establishing environments where all students are safe, feel valued, and are respected.

Teach Prosocial Behavior

"Prosocial behavior is a broad concept including any behavior that benefits others or promotes harmonious relationships," writes Bergin (2018). "It is about the quality, not the quantity of interactions with others. . . . Prosocial behavior includes kindness, compassion, collaboration, teamwork, and cooperation, but none of these behaviors alone encompasses prosocial behavior" (p. 14). Teaching prosocial behavior means more than teaching students to be nice; it also means promoting social justice and harmony. Research shows that teaching prosocial behavior can lead not only to better classroom management, but also to increased academic achievement for students (Sinclair et al., 2021; Wiedermann et al., 2020).

Misbehaviors are opportunities both for individual student growth and for the development of a classroom community, but building a community begins with teachers relinquishing the urge to have instant control. Instead of handing down a simple verdict, we encourage teachers to view this as a problem-solving opportunity for the student. Rather than public shaming or instant punishment, begin with a private conversation. Start by acknowledging that there is a problem, then let the student define it. Ask the student to describe why it poses a problem. Then, let the student think and talk through how to best resolve the problem. Let the student try to fix it, and offer help if they need it. Arrange for a time in the day when the student can come back and give you an update on how things are going.

Focus on the Co-Creation of a Peaceful Community

The book *Starting Small* (Teaching Tolerance Project, 2008) includes a chapter dedicated to helping children practice creating a peaceful community. In it, the authors describe a teacher, Lourdes Ballesteros-Barron, who made peacemaking a priority in her kindergarten classroom through the use of a "Peace Table":

> One area of the classroom is set aside for a special purpose. The Peace Table is these kindergartners' summit site, a private,

> neutral setting for negotiating differences. To help with the difficult task of voicing uncomfortable feelings and listening respectfully, the problem-solvers have a menagerie of hand puppets to choose from. Two small chairs keep the proceedings simple, one-to-one. The table is covered in bright cloth and backed by a bulletin board that displays photographs of children from earlier Peace Table sessions. The photos let the children know that peacemaking is a time-honored activity here. (p. 64)

The nonprofit organization Learning for Justice (learningforjustice.org), formerly Teaching Tolerance, offers schools access to a free DVD containing video of a classroom "peace summit" where two children work through a disagreement. Although the video is not available for streaming as we write this, it can be requested at no cost from the organization's website. It is remarkable to watch how 5-year-olds can be equipped with strategic conversational tools to "make peace." When there is an interpersonal conflict, both students get to address the infraction, and both of them walk away feeling better about themselves and each other. We often tell young children to "use your words" but often fail to recognize that this is hard to do, particularly when the only words they have are angry words. The power behind the Peace Table is that the students' conversations are scaffolded using the following prompts, which are posted at the table for students to reference:

1. Identify the problem.
2. Focus on the problem.
3. Attack the problem, not the person.
4. Listen with an open mind.
5. Treat a person's feelings with respect.
6. Take responsibility for your actions. (Teaching Tolerance Project, 2008, p. 68)

In addition, students who struggle talking directly to another person can instead role-play using puppets.

With the Peace Table strategy, teachers don't ignore student infractions, but they don't solve the problem for students either. They simply ask, "Would it help if you went to the Peace Table?" (p. 74). There's a powerful goal of redemption and restoration in the process of participating in peace talks. The goal isn't punishment. Instead, "if someone does something wrong, we talk to them and help them to do it right" (p. 64).

The 2x10 Strategy

Angela Watson (2014) writes the popular blog *The Cornerstone for Teachers.* Several years ago, she wrote a brief blog entry that we have made required reading for all our students ever since. Crediting Raymond Wlodkowski with the original idea, she explains what she calls the "2x10" strategy: "Spend 2 minutes per day for 10 days in a row talking with an at-risk student about anything she or he wants to talk about." That's it! The comments on her blog provide anecdotal evidence of the power of the strategy to reform hard-to-reach students. Our student teacher candidates have also reported remarkable success with this simple formula.

Gerry Brooks (2019) tells a similar story of a kindergarten student who thrived on being the center of attention. "I told her teacher, 'You handle her so well.' The teacher told me, 'At the beginning of the day, I let her come up, and I give her two minutes of carpet time to do whatever she wants. She'll sing a song; she'll do a dance. She gets the attention of the entire class, and then we move on. She loves it.' The teacher was able to give that child what she needed in order to get through the day" (p. 73). The simple 2x10 strategy requires no money, training, or prep work, yet it has the potential to create meaningful bonds that can go a long way toward supporting community in the classroom.

Appeal to Students' Better Selves

Mrs. Royce, a 1st grade teacher, demonstrated the power of giving students the benefit of the doubt in her interactions with her students. When a child committed an infraction, Mrs. Royce would say something like, "Johnny, I know there's more to this story. We'll talk about it as soon as I'm finished here," then continue with her whole-group lesson. After getting to an appropriate place in her lesson and asking the rest of the students to work on their math activity, Mrs. Royce would call the students involved in the infraction to her table and emphasize how it would make her sad to know they had done this on purpose, which is why she didn't believe that either of them had meant to hurt the other. She'd then ask them to talk about it and come to an agreement. The students, eager to show their better selves, would then explain or apologize to each other, and go merrily on their way.

Mrs. Royce used this strategy often, providing students a way out of their shame. A knee-jerk inflicting of punishment or asking a student to change their status on the behavior chart would not have done the work of changing a student's mind or heart. Mrs. Royce provided an opportunity for students to redeem themselves. And through her modeling, she helped students believe the best about themselves and each other. Appealing to their better selves resulted in the students trying to live up to Mrs. Royce's good opinion of them. They didn't want to disappoint her. Never once did she resort to using a behavior chart. She addressed students' misbehaviors by focusing on the good in them, giving them the benefit of the doubt.

Believing in students is a powerful force for changing behaviors and developing skills. Mrs. Royce appealed to her students' better selves, and they responded by behaving like their better selves.

Thoughtfully Address Disruptions

Most teachers know that rules and structures are essential components of effective teaching in an environment where all students feel safe. But one of the biggest problems with behavior charts and withholding recess is that they do nothing to teach students how to self-regulate. Instead, behavior charts reinforce damaging beliefs, serving as a poster-sized reminder of who the "good kids" are and who the "bad kids" are. Withholding recess only exacerbates your current problem of not allowing the students who need it the most an opportunity to release pent-up energy; what's more, it denies them the chance to practice badly needed social skills within *actual* social settings.

On the other hand, we are not suggesting that you ignore disruptions. Subtle, silent actions, like a meaning-filled look or proximity (standing next to a student), can go a long way in addressing many disruptions, but there are times when you need to address a disruption decisively and publicly—for example, "Johnny, put that down, please." But once the student has stopped the behavior, rather than reflexively following up with another public direction (to adjust a behavior clip), a private conversation is a better approach. In other words, we ought to judiciously address specific situations with the specific interventions that will be most beneficial. We ought to outright teach students how to self-regulate behavior.

With that in mind, consider the motives behind your go-to consequences. Ask yourself, "Are my actions teaching this student how to self-regulate?" During your private conversation with the student, if you need to *tell* the student why the behavior was unacceptable, then do that, but if you can get the student to *tell you,* that's even better. For example, for students who are distracting their peers or interrupting your teaching, you might ask, "Can you tell me why I wanted to talk with you? Can you tell me why the way you were behaving was problematic?" Guide students who are unable to identify or articulate this toward the reasons, and help them develop a plan they can use to self-regulate more effectively. This doesn't need to take a long time. For example, you might ask, "What's something you might try in order to remind yourself to take better control of this habit?" Finally, sympathize and explain the temporary consequence—for example, "It would make me sad to have to move your desk, because I love the way you're such a good friend to your teammates." And then check back with the student, applauding progress made ("I knew you could do that") and stepping in to help solve problems where needed.

Teach Conflict Resolution

There is a pressing concern in society that we strongly believe ought to be addressed in K–12 schools. No doubt you have seen viral videos of escalating tensions, poorly handled, that have, without exaggeration, ruined or ended people's lives. As society becomes more and more tribal, as the world becomes increasingly polarized, now more than ever we need to equip our students with tools for skillfully resolving conflict before it escalates to the point of ruining lives and relationships. This is not to minimize the importance of calling out injustice. But education that is responsive to the needs of a changing world should absolutely adapt to meet this growing need, starting in kindergarten and continuing through high school.

With that in mind, we'd like to propose that schools intentionally embed *conflict resolution* as an essential component of their SEL focus. Several sources listed at the end of this chapter provide information toward that end. Skill in conflict resolution is needed not only by future counselors and therapists, but also by teachers, administrators, law enforcement personnel, politicians, grocery store workers, sidewalk citizens, and arguably every human being on the planet. By addressing this need now, maybe, just maybe, we can get to a point where we'll be able to celebrate the day when the content is no longer as desperately needed.

Explore and Employ SEL Resources

Any number of books exist that can help you foster healthy social and emotional environments in your classroom. The following websites also provide free SEL support:

- **The Collaborative for Academic, Social, and Emotional Learning (CASEL; www.casel.org).** CASEL's website is a good place to start, providing a plethora of practical resources including needs-assessment guides and implementation guides for students at all levels, from preschool through high school.
- **The Wallace Foundation (www.wallacefoundation.org).** The Wallace Foundation provides a free, downloadable 400-page resource called "Navigating Social and Emotional Learning from the Inside Out," developed in collaboration with the Harvard Graduate School of Education. This resource takes you inside 25 successful programs, providing guidance on curriculum, content, and program development.
- **The ASCD Whole Child Network (www.ascd.org).** Even before SEL became common educational lingo, ASCD had embarked on an initiative focused on providing resources for designing environments that ensure that each student is healthy, safe, engaged, supported, and challenged. The initiative has since become the ASCD Whole Child Network—a global community providing tools and resources for creating supportive schools. Registration is free.
- **The Aspen Institute (www.aspeninstitute.org).** For those interested in reviewing the Aspen Institute's final report on the power of SEL, it is available as a free download on their website. This

report includes voices from scientists, educators, and policymakers and provides a helpful "road map for change."

Conclusion

We tend to address student misbehaviors in the same way our misbehaviors were addressed when we were children. These knee-jerk responses, such as those inherent in behavior charts and withholding recess, feel like they would be effective and logical consequences to student misbehaviors. But they often lead to repeated or worse behaviors.

Much of what we write about in this book deals with practices that work in the short term but end up costing in terms of long-term losses or practices that serve to exacerbate the issues surrounding the initial problem they were meant to fix. Conversely, restorative practices and approaches that address the social and emotional learning needs of children are not quick fixes. They take an investment of will and time, but pay off in the long term by benefiting our students and ultimately improving the classroom environment.

Conclusion

Leave the gun. Take the cannoli.
The Godfather, 1972

Parenting is a joyful experience, but it's also filled with fears, failures, and occasional regrets. Our friend Jenn was once trying to write a cheerful message on a "new baby" greeting card. With an anguished look on her face, she asked, "Should I tell them the truth?" We laughed because, as parents, we knew exactly what she was talking about. The day we held our first child is the day our façade of personal control was demolished by a pudgy little ball of flesh who couldn't even hold her head up. Despite all of parenting's joys, it can be a humbling experience.

As professors of teacher education, we relate to Jenn's momentary anguish. With the news of every job placement, we feel a strong sense of excitement and pride for our bright-eyed new teachers, but in our minds, we too wonder, "Should I tell you the truth?"

Here is what that truth includes. On bad days, you won't just feel like a bad teacher; you'll feel like a bad person. Sometimes you will rise to the challenges you face, and sometimes you will fail—and it's the failures that you're bound to remember. Our goal in writing this book was certainly not to make an already humbling experience any more daunting than it is. We know that teaching is hard. Rather, we wanted to present alternatives for practices that, however well-meaning, may actually do more harm than good. It's important for all educators to recognize and remember the following:

- We all have choices.
- Our choices have side effects.
- We all need grace.
- We need one another.

We All Have Choices

Every day, we are faced with choices that can serve to either support or sabotage meaningful student learning. Angela Watson (2014) reminds us that self-empowerment begins with analyzing those choices. Teachers often have more control than we think we do, and the most effective teachers think through their options to determine what they and their students actually need in order to thrive.

For example, while none of us has the power to change the state-adopted standards, each of us has discretion as to how to help students meet those standards. We've never seen written mandates requiring the use of the traditional Q&A format or teaching to learning styles. A teacher who sets out to assess student engagement, fluency, and comprehension has many options besides round robin reading. Teaching is a creative process, so let's get creative!

Our Choices Have Side Effects

No teacher implements a strategy with the intention of *reducing* student learning. All the problematic practices discussed in this book are generally applied with the best of intentions. Yong Zhao (2018) rightly reminds us that medicines have side effects, and most medicines also have the potential of being a poison. For example, Zhao explains, "This program may improve your reading scores but may make your students hate reading forever" (2018). That's a nugget of truth we ought to continually keep in mind. When implementing a practice, ask yourself, *Why am I doing this? Does it align with what I value? Does it undermine what I believe matters most? Does it support deep and meaningful student learning?* Serving students well means critically assessing every practice you use. It's your classroom, so it's up to you to steer it in the right direction.

We All Need Grace

At some point, all of us have embraced, or will embrace, fads and practices that are less than effective. We all have made or will make choices that will make us look back and wince. Supporting the cognitive, social, and affective growth of the human beings in our classrooms is a very heavy lift! And that's why we need to give ourselves and our colleagues some grace. Instead of dwelling on mistakes, focus on solutions and pursue effective alternatives. Keep asking, *What should we change?* and *How should we change it?* And celebrate yourself and your colleagues as you evolve.

We Need One Another

Somewhere—likely within your own faculty—there are teachers who have strengths in the same areas where you have needs, and there are teachers who have needs in the same areas where you have strengths. Share your strengths, and reach out for help with your weaknesses.

When working with teachers, we often ask them to write down the number of years that they have been teaching. Each table then adds up the total number of years represented at their tables. We then go around and add up the total number of years that they have collectively, as a building, been teaching. We then post that number (which always seems to surprise teachers) in a prominent location, where it stays for the duration of our time working together. It is meant to be a reminder of the collective experiences, the collective victories, the collective tears, and the collective challenges that we've overcome. Together, we really can handle anything—including the need for change.

When we started teaching 30 years ago, nobody blinked about rules requiring female teachers to wear pantyhose with their skirts and dresses. And nobody even thought to complain about allowing every teachers' lounge to be filled with the toxic smog of cigarette smoke. We've moved on from these archaic rules and habits, which, at the time, seemed unremarkable. Likewise, we need to move on from educational practices that provide short-term gains in exchange for long-term losses. These strategies may seem harmless enough, but they come at a cost of student learning and motivation, and they undermine the goals teachers have of creating a community of learners that fosters growth and overall well-being. Our hope is that it will one day be as hard to find counterproductive practices in schools as it is to find a smoke-filled teachers' lounge today.

Acknowledgments

We are so appreciative of the support and guidance provided by Genny Ostertag and Katie Martin at ASCD. First, regarding Genny Ostertag, senior director of acquisitions and editing: too few people know the positive impact she has had on the landscape of K–12 education. Genny is knowledgeable and intuitive, and her guidance with this book was essential. Next, there is Senior Editor Katie Martin, whose insights, queries, and suggestions really did make this a better book. She combed through thousands and thousands of words and musings—deleting, moving, inserting, and deleting again. She's excellent at what she does, and we're so thankful she did it for us. We also want to thank ASCD Art Director Donald Ely, who stepped out of his usual role to create a fun and lively book cover that we love, and we thank the whole of the ASCD editorial and production team, including Ernesto Yermoli, Jennifer Morgan, Laura Larson, Christopher Logan, Keith Demmons, and Shajuan Martin. And we thank Stefani Roth, former publisher at ASCD. Her understanding of the needs in K–12 education and her dedication to making it better has left a lasting and positive mark on schools. We are glad to have had the opportunity to work with her.

Thank you to our reviewers: Philip Bassett, Denise Bender, Anita de la Isla, Karla Gibson, Ann Hummel, Mary Iovino, Keely Potter, Carmen Rowe, Jennifer Schnabel, and Jenny Swecker. They are teachers and educational leaders whom we also count as friends. They counseled us and provided us with opportunities for reflection. Their feedback was needed and welcomed. And we're thankful that they were able to lend their voices to this book.

Thank you to Alicia Denmark, Marie Grutza, and Mel Clingan—former students who are now serving as excellent teachers in their own classrooms—and to Kayla Wenger, a current student who is on her way to becoming an excellent teacher. We also want to thank elementary school principal Camille Hopkins, who provided input and direction for this book. These teachers and leaders let us "run some ideas by them" (and then another idea, and another), entertaining our phone calls, texted questions, and private messages while they were trying to relax on social media.

We also thank our amazing colleagues and friends Judy Wenrich, Lesley Colabucci, Charlton Wolfgang, Jennifer Burke, Aileen Hower, Deborah Tamakloe, Kazi Hossain, Ann Gaudino, and the faculty at Millersville University's Early, Middle, and Exceptional Education Program. They lent us their time, expertise, and books (which we may or may not return) and gave us their friendship. Sometimes, after we talked with them, we ran back to our offices to take notes. We thank them for their influence.

Finally, we are thankful to God for "chance" encounters and answered prayers.

References

Acosta, J., Chinman, M., Engberg, J., & Augustine, C. (2015). Rethinking student discipline and zero tolerance. *Education Week, 35*(8), 24.

Allington, R. (2009). *What really matters in fluency: Research-based practices across the curriculum.* Allyn & Bacon.

Allington, R. (2011, March). What at-risk readers need. *Educational Leadership, 68*(6), 40–45.

Allington, R. (2013). What really matters when working with struggling readers. *The Reading Teacher, 66*(7), 520–530.

Allington, R. (2014). How reading volume affects both reading fluency and reading achievement. *International Electronic Journal of Elementary Education, 7*(1), 13–26.

American Academy of Pediatrics. (2013). The crucial role of recess in school: Council on school health. *Pediatrics, 131*(1), 183–188.

Andrä, C., Mathias, B., Schwager, A., Macedonia, M., & von Kriegsteirn, K. (2020). Learning foreign language vocabulary with gestures and pictures enhances vocabulary memory for several months post-learning in eight-year-old school children. *Educational Psychology Review, 32,* 815–850.

Ash, G., Kuhn, M. R., & Walpole, S. (2009). Analyzing "inconsistencies" in practice: Teachers' continued use of round robin oral reading. *Reading & Writing Quarterly, 25*(1), 87–103.

Aspen Institute. (2019). *From a national at risk to a national at hope: Recommendations from the National Commission on Social, Emotional, & Academic Development.* https://nationathope.org/wp-content/uploads/2018_aspen_final-report_full_webversion.pdf

Barbe, W. B., Swassing, R. H., & Milone, M. N. (1979). *Teaching through modality strengths: Concepts and practices.* Zaner-Bloser.

Belfield, C., Bowden, A., Klapp, A., Levin, H., Shand, R., & Zander, S. (2015). The economic value of social and emotional learning. *Journal of Benefit-Cost Analysis, 6*(3), 508–544.

Bennett, S., & Kalish, N. (2006). *The case against homework: How homework is hurting children and what parents can do about it.* Three Rivers.

Bergin, C. (2018). *Designing a prosocial classroom: Growing kinder students from pre-K–12 with the curriculum you already use.* W. W. Norton.

Biggs, M., Homan, S., Dedrick, R., & Rasinski, T. (2008). Using an interactive singing software program: A comparative study of middle school struggling readers. *Reading Psychology, 29*(3), 195–213.

Black, P., & Wiliam, D. (1998). Inside the black box: Raising standards through classroom assessment. *Phi Delta Kappan, 80*(2), 139–148.

Boser, U. (2019, September). *What do teachers know about the science of learning? A survey of educators on how students learn.* The Learning Agency. https://www.the-learning-agency.com/insights/what-do-teachers-know-about-the-science-of-learning

Brackett, M. A. (2018, October). The emotional intelligence we owe students and educators. *Educational Leadership, 76*(2), 13–18.

Bridgeland, J., Bruce, M., & Hariharan, A., &(2013). *The missing piece: A national teacher survey on how social and emotional learning can empower children and transform schools. A report for CASEL.* Collaborative for Academic, Social, and Emotional Learning. https://casel.org/wp-content/uploads/2016/01/the-missing-piece.pdf

Britton, B. K., & Tesser, A. (1991). Effects of time-management practices on college grades. *Journal of Education Psychology, 83*(3), 405–410.

Brooks, G. (2019). *Go see the principal: True tales from the school trenches.* Da Capo.

Cassiello-Robbins, C., Wilner, J. G., Peters, J. R., Bentley, K. H., & Sauer-Zavala, S. (2019). Elucidating the relationships between shame, anger, and self-destructive behaviors: The role of aversive responses to emotions. *Journal of Contextual Behavioral Science, 12*, 7–12.

Chang, R., & Coward, F. L. (2015). More recess time, please! *Phi Delta Kappan, 97*(3), 14–17.

Cook, D. A., Thompson, W. G., Thomas, K. G., & Thomas, M. R. (2009). Lack of interaction between sensing-intuitive learning styles and problem-first versus information-first instruction: A randomized crossover trial. *Advances in Health Sciences Education, 1*, 79.

Cooley, A. H. (2018). An efficacy examination and constitutional critique of school shaming. *Ohio State Law Journal, 79*(2), 319–374.

Cooper, H. (1989, November). Synthesis of research on homework. *Educational Leadership, 47*(3), 85–91.

Cooper, H., Robinson, J. C., & Patall, E. A. (2006). Does homework improve academic achievement? A synthesis of research, 1987–2003. *Review of Educational Research, 76*(1), 1–62.

Cunningham, A. E., & Stanovich, K. E. (2001). What reading does for the mind. *Journal of Direct Instruction, 1*(2), 137–149.

Cunningham, J. W. (2001, July/August/September). The National Reading Panel report. *Reading Research Quarterly, 36*(3), 326–335.

Duffy, M. E., Twenge, J. M., & Joiner, T. E. (2019). Trends in mood and anxiety symptoms and suicide-related outcomes among U.S. undergraduates, 2007–2018: Evidence from two national surveys. *Journal of Adolescent Health, 65*(5), 590–598.

Dunn, R., Dunn, K., & Price, G. E. (1984). *Learning style inventory.* Price Systems.

Durkin, D. (1978–79). What classroom observations reveal about reading comprehension instruction. *Reading Research Quarterly, 14,* 481–533.

Durkin, D. (1981, March). Schools don't teach comprehension. *Educational Leadership, 38*(6), 453–454.

Durlak, J. A., Dymnicki, A. B, Taylor, R. D., Weissberg, R. P., & Schellinger, K. B. (2011). The impact of enhancing students' social and emotional learning: A meta-analysis of school-based interventions. *Child Development, 82*(1), 405–432.

Dweck, C. S. (2006). *Mindset: The new psychology of success.* Ballantine Books.

Ebersbach, M., Feierabend, M., & Nazari, K. B. B. (2020). Comparing the effects of generating questions, testing, and restudying on students' long-term recall in university learning. *Applied Cognitive Psychology, 34,* 724–736.

Edmondson, J., & Shannon, P. (2002). Politics of reading: The will of the teacher. *The Reading Teacher, 55*(5), 452–454.

Eldredge, J. L., Reutzel, D. R., & Hollingsworth, P. M. (1996). Comparing the effectiveness of two oral reading practices: Round-robin reading and the shared book experience. *Journal of Literacy Research, 28*(2), 201–225.

Elley, W. B. (1989). Vocabulary acquisition from listening to stories. *Reading Research Quarterly, 24*(2), 174–187.

Elley, W. B. (1991, September). Acquiring literacy in a second language: The effect of book-based programs. *Language Learning, 41*(3), 375–411.

Elley, W. B. (2000, July). The potential of book floods for raising literacy levels. *International Review of Education, 46*(3/4), 233–255.

Evans, B. P., Shively, C. T. (2019). Using the Cornell Note-Taking System can help eighth grade students alleviate the impact of interruptions while reading at home. *Journal of Inquiry and Action in Education, 10*(1), 1–35.

Evans, K., & Vaandering, D. (2016). *The little book of restorative justice in education: Fostering responsibility, healing, and hope in* schools. Good Books.

Fair, G. C., & Combs, D. (2011). Nudging fledgling teen readers from the nest: From round robin to real reading. *Clearing House, 84*(5), 224–230.

Fleming, N. D., & Mills, C. (1992). Not another inventory, rather a catalyst for reflection. *To Improve the Academy,* 246. https://digitalcommons.unl.edu/podimproveacad/246/

Flood, J., Lapp, D., & Fisher, D. (2005). Neurological impress method plus. *Reading Psychology, 2,* 147.

Furey, W. (2020). The stubborn myth of "learning styles." *Education Next, 20*(3), 8–12.

Gallagher, K. (2009). *Readicide: How schools are killing reading and what you can do about it.* Stenhouse.

Galloway, M., Conner, J., & Pope, D. (2013). Nonacademic effects of homework in privileged high-performing high schools. *Journal of Experimental* Education, *81*(4), 490–510.

Gambrell, L. (2011, Fall). Motivation in the school reading curriculum. *Journal of Reading Education, 37*(1), 5–14.

Gambrell, L. B., Wilson, R. M., & Gantt, W. N. (2001). Classroom observations of task-attending behaviors of good and poor readers. *Journal of Educational Research, 74*(6), 400–404.

Garan, E. M., & DeVoogd, G. (2008). The benefits of sustained silent reading: Scientific research and common sense converge. *The Reading Teacher, 62*(4), 336–344.

Gardner, D. P. (1983). *A nation at risk: The imperative for educational reform.* National Commission on Excellence in Education.

Gill, B. P., & Schlossman, S. L. (2004). Villain or savior? The American discourse on homework, 1850–2003. *Theory into Practice, 43*(3), 174–181.

Graham, S., & Hebert, M. (2010). *Writing to read: Evidence for how writing can improve reading.* Carnegie Corporation Time to Act Report. Alliance for Excellent Education. https://www.carnegie.org/publications/writing-to-read-evidence-for-how-writing-can-improve-reading/

Graham, S., Kiuhara, S. A., & MacKay, M. (2020). The effects of writing on learning in science, social studies, and mathematics: A meta-analysis. *Review of Educational Research, 2,* 179.

Hamilton, L., Halverson, R., Jackson, S., Mandinach, E., Supovitz, J., & Wayman, J. (2009). *Using student achievement data to support instructional decision making* (NCEE 2009–4067). National Center for Education Evaluation and Regional Assistance, Institute of Education Sciences, U.S. Department of Education.

Harris, L., Wyatt-Smith, C., & Adie, L. (2020). Using data walls to display assessment results: A review of their affective impacts on teachers and students. *Teachers and Teaching, 26*(1), 50–66.

Harris, T., & Hodges, R. (Eds.). (1995). *The literacy dictionary: The vocabulary of reading and writing.* International Reading Association.

Hattie, J. (2009). *Visible learning: A synthesis of over 800 meta-analyses relating to achievement.* Routledge.

Hattie, J., & Timperley, T. (2007). The power of feedback. *Review of Educational Research, 77*(1), 81–112.

Hattie, J., & Yates, G. (2014). *Visible learning and the science of how we learn.* Routledge.

Heckelman, R. G. (1969). A neurological-impress method of remedial-reading instruction. *Academic Therapy, 4*(4), 277–282.

Henley, J., McBride, J., Milligan, J., & Nichols, J. (2007). Robbing elementary students of their childhood: The perils of No Child Left Behind. *Education, 128*(1), 56–63.

Hill, H. C. (2020, February 10). Does studying student data really raise test scores? *Education Week.* https://www.edweek.org/technology/opinion-does-studying-student-data-really-raise-test-scores/2020/02

Himmele, P., & Himmele, W. (2017). *Total participation techniques: Making every student an active learner* (2nd ed.). ASCD.

Himmele, P., Himmele, W., Hower, A., & Mackley, K. (2021, Fall). Here's what happened when we surprised our preservice teachers with a popcorn reading activity. *Pennsylvania Reads.*

Hollingsworth, P. M. (1978). An experimental approach to the impress method of teaching reading. *The Reading Teacher, 31,* 624–626.

Hurley, K. (2016, September 29). The dark side of classroom behavior charts. *Washington Post.* https://www.washingtonpost.com/news/parenting/wp/2016/09/29/the-darkside-of-classroom-behavior-management-charts/

Hyndman, B., & Wyver, S. (2020). Outdoor recreation within the school setting: A physiological and psychological exploration. In H. Nielsen (Ed.), *Outdoor recreation: Physiological and psychological effects on health* (pp. 1–17). IntechOpen London.

International Literacy Association. (2018). *The power and promise of read-alouds and independent reading* [Literacy leadership brief]. International Literacy Association. https://literacyworldwide.org/docs/default-source/where-we-stand/ila-power-promise-read-alouds-independent-reading.pdf

International Literacy Association. (2019). *Creating passionate readers through independent reading* [Literacy leadership brief]. International Literacy Association. https://www.literacyworldwide.org/docs/default-source/where-we-stand/ila-creating-passionate-readers-through-independent-reading.pdf

International Reading Association. (1999). *High-stakes assessments in reading* [Position statement]. International Reading Association. https://www.literacyworldwide.org/docs/default-source/where-we-stand/high-stakes-assessment-position-statement.pdf?sfvrsn=c44ea18e_6.

International Reading Association, Canadian Children's Book Center, & National Council of Teachers of English. (2014). *Leisure reading: A position statement of the International Reading Association* [Joint position statement]. International Reading Association. https://literacyworldwide.org/docs/default-source/where-we-stand/leisure-reading-position-statement.pdf

Jones, S. (2013). Literacies in the body. *Journal of Adolescent & Adult Literacy, 56*(7), 525–529.

Jung, L. A., & Smith, D. (2018, September). Tear down your behavior chart. *Educational Leadership, 76*(1), 12–18.

Kamenetz, A. (2015). *The test: Why our schools are obsessed with standardized testing—but you don't have to be.* Public Affairs.

Kamenetz, A. (2018, April 29). *What "A Nation at Risk" got wrong, and right, about U.S. schools* [Radio broadcast]. NPR. Thttps://www.npr.org/sections/ed/2018/04/29/604986823/what-a-nation-at-risk-got-wrong-and-right-about-u-s-schools

Kavale, K. A., & Forness, S. R. (1987). Substance over style: Assessing the efficacy of modality testing and teaching. *Exceptional Children, 54*(3), 228–239.

Kelleher, I., & Whitman, G. (2020, May 28). Every educator needs to know how the brain learns. *ASCD Express, 15*(18). http://www.ascd.org/ascd-express/vol15/num18/every-educator-needs-to-know-how-the-brain-learns.aspx

Keyes, K. M., Gary, D., O'Malley, P., Hamilton, A., & Schulenberg, J. E. (2019). Recent increases in depressive symptoms among US adolescents: Trends from 1991 to 2018. *Social Psychiatry and Psychiatric Epidemiology, 54*, 987–996.

Kohn, A. (2006a). Abusing research: The study of homework and other examples. *Phi Delta Kappan, 88*(1), 8–22.

Kohn, A. (2006b). *The homework myth: Why our kids get too much of a bad thing.* Da Capo.

Kohn, A. (2007, January/February). *Rethinking homework.* Principal. www.alfiekohn.org/article/rethinking-homework

Kohn, A. (2015). *Schooling beyond measure and other unorthodox essays about education.* Heinemann.

Koretz, D. (2017). *The testing charade: Pretending to make schools better.* University of Chicago Press.

Kowalski, M. J., & Froiland, J. M. (2020). Parent perceptions of elementary classroom management systems and their children's motivational and emotional responses. *Social Psychology of Education, 23*(2), 433–448.

Krashen, S. D. (2004). *The power of reading: Insights from the research.* Heinemann.

Krashen, S. D. (2005). Is in-school free reading good for children? Why the National Reading Panel report is (still) wrong. *Phi Delta Kappan, 86*(6), 444–447.

LaBerge, D., & Samuels, S. A. (1974). Toward a theory of automatic information processing in reading. *Cognitive Psychology, 6*, 293–323.

Lahtinen, V., Lonka, K., & Lindblom-Ylänne, S. (1997). Spontaneous study strategies and the quality of knowledge construction. *British Journal of Educational Psychology, 67*(1), 13–24.

Lapp, D., & Fisher, D. (2010). *Handbook on teaching the English language arts* (3rd ed.). Routledge.

Leahy, S., Lyon, C., Thompson, M., & Wiliam, D. (2005, November). Classroom assessment: Minute by minute, day by day. *Educational Leadership, 63*(3), 18–24.

Learning Sciences International. (2019). *The future of assessment practices: Comprehensive and balanced assessment systems: Recommendations from the National Panel on the Future of Assessment Practices* [Policy paper]. https://www.dylanwiliamcenter.com/whitepapers/assessment/

Lee, P. L., Lan, W., Hamman, D., & Hendricks, B. (2008). The effects of teaching notetaking strategies on elementary students' science learning. *Instructional Science, 36*, 191–201.

Lench, S. C. (2019, July 10). This is not a test: The real root of "assessment" will surprise you *Future Focused Education.* https://futurefocusededucation.org/2019/07/10/this-is-not-a-test-the-real-root-of-assessment-will-surprise-you/

Lewis, M., & Ramsay, D. (2002). Cortisol response to embarrassment and shame. *Child Development, 73*(4), 1034–1045.

Livingston, G. (2019, February 20). *The way U.S. teens spend their time is changing, but differences between boys and girls persist.* Pew Research Center. https://www.pewresearch.org/fact-tank/2019/02/20/the-way-u-s-teens-spend-their-time-is-changing-but-differences-between-boys-and-girls-persist/

London, R. (2019). The right to play: Eliminating the opportunity gap in elementary school recess. *Phi Delta Kappan, 101*(3), 48–52.

London, R. A., Westrich, L., Stokes-Guinan, K., & McLaughlin, M. (2015). Playing fair: The contribution of high-functioning recess to overall school climate in low-income elementary schools. *Journal of School Health, 85*(1), 53–60.

Macdonald, K., Germine, L., Anderson, A., Christodoulou, J., & McGrath, L. M. (2017). Dispelling the myth: Training in education or neuroscience decreases but does not eliminate beliefs in neuromyths. *Frontiers in Psychology, 8,* 1314.

Marzano, R. J., & Pickering, D. J. (2007). Errors and allegations about research on homework. *Phi Delta Kappan, 88*(7), 507–513.

McNamara, L., & Walker, M. (2018). "It is just too fun to explain": A qualitative analysis of the recess project in seven lower-socioeconomic elementary schools. *Canadian Journal of Action Research, 19*(2), 48–66.

McReynolds, K. (2007, Autumn). Homework: A conversation with Sara Bennett. *Encounter, 20*(3), 11–15.

Mills, R. S. L., Imm, G. P., Walling, B. R., & Weler, H. A. (2008). Cortisol reactivity and regulation associated with shame responding in early childhood. *Developmental Psychology, 44*(5), 1369–1380.

Mojtabai, R., Olfson, M., & Han, B. (2016). National trends in the prevalence and treatment of depression in adolescents and young adults. *Pediatrics, 138*(6).

Murata, A., Siker, J., Kang, B., Evra M., Baldinger, E., Kim, H. -J., Scott, M., & Lanouette, K. (2017). Math talk and student strategy trajectories: The case of two first grade classrooms. *Cognition and Instruction, 35*(4), 290–316.

Nagy, W., Herman, P. A., & Anderson, R. C. (1985). Learning words from context. *Reading Research Quarterly, 20*(2), 233–253.

National Council of Teachers of English. (1995). *Resolution on testing* [Position statement]. https://ncte.org/statement/testing/

National Council of Teachers of English. (2018). *Literacy assessment: Definitions, principles, and practices* [Position statement]. https://ncte.org/statement/assessmentframingst/print/

National Council of Teachers of English. (2019). *Statement on independent reading* [Position statement]. https://ncte.org/statement/independent-reading/print/

National Council of Teachers of Mathematics. (2016). *Large-scale mathematics and high-stakes decisions: A position of the National Council of Teachers of Mathematics* [Position statement]. https://www.nctm.org/Standards-and-Positions/Position-Statements/Large-Scale-Mathematics-Assessments-and-High-Stakes-Decisions/

National Panel on the Future of Assessment Practices. (2019). *The future of assessment practices: Comprehensive and balanced assessment systems: Recommendations from the National Panel on the Future of Assessment Practices* [Policy paper]. Learning Sciences International. https://www.dylanwiliamcenter.com/whitepapers/assessment/

National PTA. (2016). *Resolution on homework: Quality over quantity* [Position statement]. https://www.pta.org/home/advocacy/ptas-positions/Individual-PTA-Resolutions/Homework-Quality-Over-Quantity

National Reading Panel. (2000). *Teaching children to read: An evidence-based assessment of the scientific research literature on reading and its implications for reading instruction.* National Institute of Child Health and Human Development.

National Science Teachers Association. (2018). *Elementary school science* [Position statement]. https://www.nsta.org/nstas-official-positions/elementary-school-science

Neill, M. (2015, March 10). No Child Left Behind: What standardized test scores reveal about its legacy. *Washington Post.* https://www.washingtonpost.com/news/answer-sheet/wp/2015/03/10/no-child-left-behind-what-standardized-test-scores-reveal-about-its-legacy/

Ojure, L., & Sherman, T. (2001, November 28). Learning styles. *Education Week, 21*(13), 33.

Opitz, M., & Rasinski, T. (2008). *Good-bye round robin: 25 effective oral reading strategies.* Heinemann.

Paige, D. D. (2011). 16 minutes of "eyes-on-text" can make a difference: Whole-class choral reading as an adolescent fluency strategy. *Reading Horizons, 51*(1), 1–20.

Pak, S. S., & Weseley, A. J. (2012). The effect of mandatory reading logs on children's motivation to read. *Journal of Research in Education, 22*(1), 251–265.

Palincsar, A. S., & Brown, A. L. (1984). Reciprocal teaching of comprehension-fostering and comprehension-monitoring activities. *Cognition and Instruction, 1*(2), 117–175.

Pashler, H., Bain, P., Bottge, B., Graesser, A., Koedinger, K., McDaniel, M., & Metcalfe, J. (2007). *Organizing instruction and study to improve student learning (NCER 2007–2004).* National Center for Education and Research, Institute of Education Sciences, U.S. Department of Education.

Pashler, H., McDaniel, M., Rohrer, D., Bjork, R. (2008). Learning styles: Concepts and evidence. *Psychological Science in the Public Interest, 9*(3), 105–119.

Pellegrini, A. D., & Bjorklund, D. F. (1997). The role of recess in children's cognitive performance. *Educational Psychologist, 32*(1), 35–40.

Perry, B. D. (2004, September 23). *Maltreatment and the developing child: How early childhood experience shapes child and culture.* Lecture delivered at the London Family Court Clinic, London, ON, Canada.

Pinsker, J. (2019, March 28). *The cult of homework.* The Atlantic. https://www.theatlantic.com/education/archive/2019/03/homework-research-how-much/585889/

Popham, W. J. (2018). *Assessment literacy for educators in a hurry.* ASCD.

Popham, W. J. (2019). *Classroom assessment: What teachers need to know* (9th ed.). Pearson Education.

Pressman, R. M., Sugarman, D. B., Nemon, M. L., Desjarlais, J., Owens, J. A., & Schettini-Evans, A. (2015). Homework and family stress: With consideration of parent's self-confidence, education level, and cultural background. *American Journal of Family Therapy, 43*(4), 297–313.

Professional Learning Supports. (2014). *John Hattie: Homework and its value* [Video]. Vimeo. https://vimeo.com/88093168

Ransinski, T. (2011). The art and science of teaching reading fluency. In D. Lapp & D. Fisher (Eds.), *Handbook of research on teaching the English Language Arts, 3rd edition* (238–247). Routledge.

Rasinski, T. (2012). Why reading fluency should be hot. *The Reading Teacher, 65*(8), 516–522.

Rasinski, T., & Padak, N. (Eds.). (2013). *From fluency to comprehension: Powerful instruction through authentic reading.* Guilford Press.

Ravitch, D. (2020, February 1). *The education reform movement has failed America. We need common sense solutions that work.* Time. https://time.com/5775795/education-reform-failed-america/

Reinke, W. M., Herman, K.C., & Newcomer, L. (2016). The brief student–teacher classroom interaction observation: Using dynamic indicators of behaviors in the classroom to predict outcomes and inform practice. *Assessment for Effective Intervention, 42*(1), 32–42.

Reutzel, D. R., & Cooter, R. B., Jr. (2019). *Teaching children to read: The teacher makes the difference.* Pearson Education.

Richardson, J. (December 2009/January 2010). Playing "catch-up" with developing nations makes no sense for U.S.: An interview with Yong Zhao. *Phi Delta Kappan, 91*(4), 15–20. https://doi.org/10.1177/003172171009100404

Roberts, J. A., Olcott, A. N., McLean, N. M., Baker, G. S., & Moller, A. (2018). Demonstrating the impact of classroom transformation on the inequality in DFW rates ("D" or "F" or withdraw) for first-time freshmen, females, and underrepresented minorities through a decadal study of introductory geology courses. *Journal of Geoscience Education, 66*(4), 304–318.

Robinson, K. (2013). *How to escape education's Death Valley* [Video]. TED Conferences. https://www.ted.com/talks/sir_ken_robinson_how_to_escape_education_s_death_valley?language=en

Robinson, K., & Aronica, L. (2018, April 19). How much homework is enough? Depends who you ask. *Education Week.* https://www.edweek.org/ew/articles/2018/04/19/how-much-homework-is-enough-depends-who.html?print=1

Rodríguez-Fernández, J. E., Pereira, V., Condessa, I., & Pereira, B. (2020). Valor atribuido al recreo escolar por el alumnado de 1 ciclo de enseñanza básica en Portugal. *Retos, 38,* 188–195.

Rohrer, D., & Pashler, H. (2012). Learning styles: Where's the evidence? *Medical Education, 46*(7), 634–635.

Russell, W. T. (2016, September 13). *Column: Hey, teachers, please stop using behavior charts. Here's why.* PBS News Hour. https://www.pbs.org/newshour/education/column-hey-teachers-please-stop-using-behavior-charts-heres

Sadoski, M., & Paivio, A. (2012). *Imagery and text: A dual coding theory of reading and writing.* Taylor & Francis.

Sanchez, C. (2013, April 26). *30 years on, educators still divided on scathing schools report* [Radio broadcast]. NPR. https://www.npr.org/2013/04/26/179281961/30-years-on-educators-still-divided-on-scathing-schools-report

Sanden, S. (2014). Out of the shadow of SSR: Real teachers' classroom independent reading practices. *Language Arts, 91*(3), 161.

Sasser, A. [@MrsSasser]. (2018, August 27). *Two years ago, I was saying "do you have any questions?". Last year I switched to "what question do you have?"* [Tweet]. Twitter. https://twitter.com/mrssasser/status/103411886135495065

Schmoker, M. (2018). *Focus: Elevating the essentials to radically improve student learning* (2nd ed.). ASCD.

Scholastic. (2019). *Kids and family reading report* (7th ed.). https://www.scholastic.com/readingreport/navigate-the-world.html

Shanahan, T. (2005). *The national reading panel report: Practical advice for teachers.* Learning Point Associates.

Shanahan, T. (2014). How and how not to prepare students for the new tests. *The Reading Teacher, 68*(3), 184–188.

Shanahan, T. (2015, April 27). Round robin by any other name . . . oral reading for older readers. *Shanahan on Literacy.* https://www.readingrockets.org/blogs/shanahan-on-literacy/round-robin-any-other-name-oral-reading-older-readers

Shanahan, T. (2019, July 29). Is round robin reading really that bad? *Shanahan on Literacy.* https://www.shanahanonliteracy.com/blog/is-round-robin-reading-really-that-bad

Simonton, K. L., & Garn, A. C. (2020). Negative emotions as predictors of behavioral outcomes in middle school physical education. *European Physical Education Review, 26*(4), 764–781.

Sinclair, J., Herman, K. C., Reinke, W. M., Dong, N., & Stormont, M. (2021). Effects of a universal classroom management intervention on middle school students with or at risk of behavior problems. *Remedial & Special Education, 42*(1), 18–30.

Smith, D., Fisher, D., & Frey, N. (2015). *Better than carrots or sticks: Restorative practices for positive classroom management.* ASCD.

Sommer, F., Leuschner, V., Fiedler, N., Madfis, E., & Scheithauer, H. (2020, March–April). The role of shame in development trajectories towards severe targeted school violence: An in-depth multiple case study. *Aggression and Violent Behavior, 51.*

Soukup, R. (2020). High, low, and interesting: A family dinner conversation game. *Living Well, Spending Less.* https://www.livingwellspendingless.com/high-low-and-interesting/

Stapp, A. C., & Karr, J. K. (2018). Effect of recess on fifth grade students' time on-task in an elementary classroom. *International Electronic Journal of Elementary Education, 10*(4), 449–456.

Stiggins, R. J., & Chappuis, J. (2006). What a difference a word makes: Assessment FOR learning rather than assessment OF learning helps students succeed. *Journal of Staff Development, 27*(1), 10–14.

Strauss, V. (2019, October 30). The education conversation we should be having. *The Washington Post.* https://www.washingtonpost.com/education/2019/10/30/education-conversation-we-should-be-having/

Taylor, R. D., Oberle, E., Durlak, J. A., & Weissberg, R. P. (2017). Promoting positive youth development through school-based social and emotional learning interventions: A meta-analysis of follow-up effects. *Child Development, 88*(4), 1156–1171.

Teaching Tolerance Project. (2008). *Starting small: Teaching tolerance in preschool and the early grades* (3rd ed.). Southern Poverty Law Center. https://www.learningforjustice.org/sites/default/files/kits/Teachers_ Study_Guide.pdf

Tenenbaum, H. R., Winstone, N .E., Leman, P. J., & Avery, R. E. (2020). How effective is peer interaction in facilitating learning? A meta-analysis. *Journal of Educational Psychology, 112*(7), 1303–1319.

Terada, Y. (2018, February 23). *What's the right amount of homework?* Edutopia. https://www.edutopia.org/article/whats-right-amount-homework

Thrower, A. (2019, November 6). *Ditching the reading logs.* Edutopia. https://www.edutopia.org/article/ditching-reading-logs

Tyner, A., & Kabourek, S. (2020). *Social studies instruction and reading comprehension: Evidence from the early childhood longitudinal study.* Thomas B. Fordham Institute. https://fordhaminstitute.org/national/resources/social-studies-instruction-and-reading-comprehension

Vatterott, C. (2018). *Rethinking homework: Best practices that support diverse needs.* ASCD.

Venable, S. (2017). Recess and academic achievement. *National Teacher Education Journal, 10*(1), 75–78.

Watson, A. (2014). The 2x10 Strategy: A miraculous solution for behavior issues? *The Cornerstone for Teachers.* https://thecornerstoneforteachers.com/the-2x10-strategy-a-miraculous-solution-for-behavior-issues/

West, M. R., & Schwerdt, G. (2012). The middle school plunge. *Education Next, 12*(2), 62–68.

Wexler, N. (2019, December 3). *The roots of teenagers' mediocre test scores lie in elementary school.* Forbes. https://www.forbes.com/sites/nataliewexler/2019/12/03/the-roots-of-teenagers-mediocre-test-scores-lie-in-elementary-school

Wiedermann, W., Reinke, W. M., & Herman, K. C. (2020). Prosocial skills causally mediate the relation between effective classroom management and academic competence: An application of direction dependence analysis. *Development Psychology, 56*(9), 1723–1735.

Wiggins, G., & McTighe, J. (2005). *Understanding by design* (2nd ed.). ASCD.

Wiliam, D. (2007). Content then process: Teacher learning communities in the service of formative assessment. In D. Reeves (Ed.), *Ahead of the curve: The power of assessment to transform teaching and learning* (pp. 183–206). Solution Tree.

Willingham, D. (2005). Ask the cognitive scientist: Do visual, auditory, and kinesthetic learners need visual, auditory, and kinesthetic instruction? *American Federation of Teachers.* https://www.aft.org/ae/summer2005/willingham

Willingham, D. (2015). The scientific status of learning styles theories. *Teaching of Psychology, 42*(3), 266–271.

Willingham, D. (2018, Summer). Ask the cognitive scientist: Does tailoring instruction to "learning styles" help students learn? *American Federation of Teachers.* https://www.aft.org/ae/summer2018/willingham

Wisniewski, B., & Zierer, K., & Hattie, J. (2020, January 22). The power of feedback revisited: A meta-analysis of educational feedback research. *Frontiers in Psychology.* https://doi.org/10.3389/fpsyg.2019.03087

Young, C., Pearce, D., Gomez, J., Christensen, R., Pletcher, B., & Fleming, K. (2018). Read two impress and the neurological impress method: Effects on elementary students' reading fluency, comprehension, and attitude. *Journal of Education Research, 11*(96), 657–665.

Zehr, H. (2004). Commentary: Restorative justice: Beyond victim-offender mediation. *Conflict Resolution Quarterly, 22*(1–2), 305–315.

Zhao, Y. (2009). *Catching up or leading the way: American education in the age of globalization*. ASCD.

Zhao, Y. (2015, April). A world at risk: An imperative for a paradigm shift to cultivate 21st century learners. *Society, 2,* 129–135. https://doi.org/10.1007/s12115-015-9872-8

Zhao, Y. (2018). *What works may hurt: Side effects in education*. Teachers College Press.

Index

The letter *f* following a page number denotes a figure.

About the Authors

Pérsida Himmele and **William (Bill) Himmele** have conducted hundreds of professional development seminars in the United States and around the world and have written six books on the topics of increasing student engagement, teaching English learners, and literacy development. ASCD has published four of their books, including the bestseller *Total Participation Techniques: Making Every Student an Active Learner,* along with two Quick Reference Guides.

The Himmeles have been married for more than 30 years. They met in college, graduated together with their PhDs, hooded each other on stage, and even shared a kiss before being politely escorted off (read: aggressively escorted off) by commencement personnel.

Prior to becoming a professor of teacher education at Millersville University, Pérsida was an elementary and middle school bilingual and multilingual classroom teacher. She also served as a district English language learner program administrator. Pérsida is Puerto Rican and is allergic to dogs, but she owns one anyway because life is better with dogs. Her

Twitter handle is @persidahimmele, and her Pokémon Go trainer code is 2159 6288 2936.

Prior to becoming an associate professor of teacher education at Millersville University, Bill was a speech teacher and an ESL teacher, and he has served as a university ESL certificate program coordinator. Bill loves scuba diving and exploring wildlife. He is a hopeless Buffalo Sabres and Buffalo Bills fan. (*Shhh. We know.*) He has life-sized cutouts of superheroes in his office, and his favorite game of all time is Red Dead Redemption 2.

Pérsida and Bill have two children, who are surprisingly well-balanced, and a three-legged rescue dog named BoBo. For those who are curious, the name *Himmele* rhymes with *simile.* Their website, TotalParticipation Techniques.com, has lots of free resources for teachers.

Related ASCD Resources: Teaching

At the time of publication, the following resources were available (ASCD stock numbers in parentheses):

The 12 Touchstones of Good Teaching: A Checklist for Staying Focused Every Day by Bryan Goodwin and Elizabeth Ross Hubbell (#113009)

Assessment Literacy for Educators in a Hurry by W. James Popham (#119009)

Classroom Instruction That Works: Research-Based Strategies for Increasing Student Achievement, 2nd Edition by Ceri B. Dean, Elizabeth Ross Hubbell, Howard Pitler, and Bj Stone (#111001)

A Handbook for Classroom Instruction That Works, 2nd Edition by Howard Pitler & Bj Stone (#112013)

The Highly Effective Teacher: 7 Classroom-Tested Practices That Foster Student Success by Jeff Marshall (#117001)

Never Work Harder Than Your Students and Other Principles of Great Teaching, 2nd Edition by Robyn R. Jackson (#118034)

So Each May Soar: The Principles and Practices of Learner-Centered Classrooms by Carol Ann Tomlinson (#118006)

Teach, Reflect, Learn: Building Your Capacity for Success in the Classroom by Pete Hall and Alisa Simeral (#115040)

Teaching in the Fast Lane: How to Create Active Learning Experiences by Suzy Pepper Rollins (#117024)

Total Participation Techniques: Making Every Student an Active Learner, 2nd Edition by Persida Himmele and William Himmele (#117033)

What We Say and How We Say It Matter: Teacher Talk That Improves Student Learning and Behavior by Mike Anderson (#119024)

For up-to-date information about ASCD resources, go to www.ascd.org. You can search the complete archives of *Educational Leadership* at www.ascd.org/el.

For more information, send an email to member@ascd.org; call 1-800-933-2723 or 703-578-9600; send a fax to 703-575-5400; or write to Information Services, ASCD, 1703 N. Beauregard St., Alexandria, VA 22311-1714 USA.